Responsibility and Accounting

the organizational regulation of boundary conditions

Responsibility and Accounting

the organizational regulation of
boundary conditions

A mid-century production for
Sten Jönsson

Editors:
Thomas Polesie
Inga-Lill Johansson

British Library Cataloguing in Publication Data
A catalogue record for this book is available from the British Library

ISBN 91-44-36091-6 Studentlitteratur
ISBN 0-86238-306-4 Chartwell Bratt Ltd
© Thomas Polesie, Inga-Lill Johansson and Studentlitteratur 1992
Printed in Sweden
Studentlitteratur, Lund

Printing:		1	2	3	4	5	6	7	8	9	10	1996	95	94	93	92

Preface

The impulse for this book came in 1990, when Sten Jönsson was about to turn fifty years of age. This was a good occasion to consider what is going on in our field of interest. We wanted to give Sten something and it seemed natural to write a book - as friends and colleagues did for his predecessors Sandor Asztély and Albert ter Vehn.

In response to a call for papers we received 11 contributions in English and 10 in Swedish. These now make up two volumes - one in each language. Taken together, they give an overview of what is going on in the accounting field as we make it out from the Gothenburg horizon. This panorama will no doubt lead on to further dialouge. After all, that is our task - to make statements, present evidence, question it and go on to making new statements.

We have worked with Sten in the past and expect to continue working with him for a long time, so we have good reason to indicate some themes of interest for further semi-confusing conversations. Each author has written about his particular area of interest - as always. Taken together, the papers develop some current issues and trains of thought. One may well wonder where these paths will take us as we follow on them.

Part 1 looks at some assumptions about the rationality of what people do. The process of communicating information about the economic aspects of an enterprise is often based on tacit assumptions that are not made quite explicit to the people involved. From time to time we all make an effort to get some understanding of how we think and don't think. Both contributions are set up as Jönssoniana - comments on Sten's work.

Jacob Birnberg's comparative essay makes an assessment of Hedberg & Jönsson's paper about semi-confusing information systems. It is placed along with Ouchi's analysis of how individuals make decisions that benefit their 'clan' and Demski & Feltham's use of agency theory as a model of the budget process.

Ezzamel & Willmott take Jönsson & Grönlund's work as their point of departure for exploring the dynamics of trust relations. They consider the extent to which the mobilization of trust for purposes of economic efficiency is constrained and enabled by the moral-political organisation in which trust is 'won.' This theme is central for grasping the contingent conditions for developing local accounting systems in different settings.

Jönsson & Grönlund's two cases illustrate that accounting systems are used to produce information for central managers rather than local employees. They lead on to the conclusion that to make information systems more relevant for local managers requires the active co-operation of the foremen and operatives in the Volvo-factory and the managers and staff of the caring establishments in the municipal study. This is easier to propose than to accomplish and presents a new set of challenges for managerial accounting.

Part 2 considers the scientific enterprise and outlines the evolution of theories within it and about it. The domain of accounting thought has now become wide indeed. There are tendencies to extend the scope of these studies until they no longer relate to traditional accounting as it was taught and known of old. Organizational theory has had a great impact and the metaphors of discourse are more far-reaching than before- and yet - beneath the shining surface of innovation there is an underlying need for continuity as a basis for coherent evaluations, judgments of policy, decision-making and action.

In 'The Engine of Inquiry' Richard Boland looks into the conceptual conditions for interpreting speech-acts. His subject is the spirit of inquiry and he explores some of its metaphors by bringing to life the conditions for dialogue. His essay contrasts the idioms used by experts, who go deep into their subject matter and those of novices. The former have elaborate cognitive structures that permit them to define problems well. The latter prefer to stay on the surface, where conflicts are not always in the foreground.

Insight into such schemas of presentation and a distinct focus on the terms of argument in use can give us a better understanding of how accounts are moulded in their characteristic forms in order to become bearers of the meanings that they are used to convey. Textual and contextual analyses of this kind sharpen the perspective of a potential 'inside-informer' by increasing the conceptual awareness of what goes on in the processes of communication or non-communication.

Much inspiration may be weaned from the efforts and experiences of other social scientists. Barbara Czarniawska-Joerges reports on findings from the field of social anthropology that have bearing on organizational theory. Her point of departure is that organization has become an essential aspect of the modern, Western, way of life. So far, organization theory has drawn heavily on the heritage of economics, political science and sociology and it will move still further afield as the social sciences free themselves from the self-imposed slavery of the natural sciences. This is a time for encounters and new horizons. Accounting can be one of them.

Using a 'Temporal System Metaphor' Rolf Lundin examines the conditions for interactive research projects. Based on a study of renewal in a family-owned business he looks into the different relationships and commitments that are set up, maintained and eventually dissolved in such projects. Interactive approaches are a speciality of corporate studies in Scandinavia. In our environment it is quite natural to conduct research projects in this way for the simple reason that we regard most other projects as interactive endeavours.

Part 3 presents studies that illustrate how networks of restrictions may be outlined and how they affect social interaction in and between organizations. A hall-mark of good accounting is the persistent effort to make clearly visible the networks of restrictions that apply. A basic theme is to study systems of accounting as man-made artefacts that are designed by someone and then taken up for use by someone else. Close observations of how these systems are handled may lead on to conclusions about how to improve them.

In action research the scientist plays a direct part in the design and conduct of experiments with system lay-out and implementation. Carmona & Gutierrez have made such an experiment at a Spanish subsidiary of a multinational car manufacturer. A local information system was designed for measuring quality cost and lead time. This study is parallel to Jönsson & Grönlund's work at Volvo's plant in Floby. The aim of the Spanish study was to analyze the conditions for designing a local information system and to examine its flexibility at different organizational levels.

Olof Arwidi looks into internal pricing in a corporate context, where 'talk' and conflicts are factors to be considered. Quite often there are markets within a corporation where prices have to be determined in some way. The chief focus of the essay is the determination of internal prices between dependent units in an organization with limited opportunities for choice of suppliers and buyers and where there are no comparable external prices.

The pricing problem is illustrated with observations at a given point in time and the model is then extended to show what happens as the conditions for trade and production change over time. This analytical approach may be supplemented by studies of pricing policies under protracted processes of structural change and extreme circumstances, where there are abrupt changes in the external environment.

Part 4 looks at how companies develop their policies. Managerial judgment is the underlying theme in Thomas Polesie's study of how companies have developed over time. The various paths they have followed - their recipes - are analyzed with regard to continuity and change, policy issues, economic performance, preoccupation with growth, internal and external conditions for communication and the evolution of corporate identity.

The evidence of how managers work under different circumstances has served as a ground for comparisons and the generation of explanations and theories about why managers do what they do. The closure that is needed for mental efforts, deliberation about policies and the requirements for disclosure and accountability are recurring themes in the analyses of how information has been generated, presented and used.

One of the basic schemes of analysis explores the distinction between action and finance as dialectically related aspects of the corporate scene. The concluding synthesis sums up some of the experiences of trying to read the corporate mind. Mental, physical and financial resources are essential categories that have emerged in the considerations of corporate policies.

Bengt Johannisson characterizes enterpreneurs as people who take initiatives, face uncertainty, and grasp opportunities. His essay illustrates how enterpreneurs make use of ambiguity as they operate both as anarchists and organizers. They challenge existing patterns of meaning and try to establish patterns of their own.

Established actors in the market tend to strive for uncertainty reduction and cost management while entrepreneurs seek opportunities and are willing to take risks. Ultimately, the process of destruction and re-creation implies a manipulation of institutionalized constructions of reality.

To bring new images of reality on stage implies competition in alien and hostile environments. This calls for experiental learning, where gains and losses that are incurred hopefully combine and give success. In order to learn experientially and to impose a new order on others, the entrepreneur must have self-confidence. The image of self is refueled through the rationalization of actions taken, whether they have been successful or not. This rationalization process calls for versatile tools, such as equivocal verbal actions and a reliable personal network. Entrepreneurs fulfill their function as managers of ambiguity in the marketplace by adopting similar vehicles for the management of their own venturing process.

Part 5 takes a look at changes in information technology and envisages some of its consequences. Ims & Grönhaug try to strike a happy medium between the adoption of new technologies and the need to maintain a creative dialogue among people.

Companies adopt new information technologies to enhance their effectiveness. They conceive of these as integral parts of their organization. Before a company actually does become more effective, the new information that has becomes available must be understood and used in adequate ways. An active dialogue has an important role to play in creating the insight and understanding that is required for ascertaining which activities really lead on to valuable results.

In the concluding essay Alf Sandin takes a look back into history. He has browsed through the centuries to find some of our accounting roots.

As Sten Jönsson was turning 50 winters, we were quite naturally reminded of another historical highlight - 500 years with Luca Pacioli. Sten Jönsson is well known, but who was Luca Pacioli? By means of a somewhat commented curriculum vitae, Alf makes us a little more acquainted with him. In spite of being a man of the church, a Franciscan, Luca Pacioli became a father. We know him as the father of double-entry book-keeping, but our account shows that he was important in other fields as well.

We will end our preface on this note, by reminding Sten to look fearlessly and cheerfully into the future. These papers honour Sten as an innovative thinker and a stimulating teacher. His work, of course, is far from done, and we look forward to honouring his next milestone - perhaps 2040?

We are grateful to the School of Economics and Commercial Law, Gothenburg University, the Foundation of Gothenburg School of Economics and Gothenburg Management Institute, for their financial support of the publishing of this volume.

Gothenburg, October 1991

Thomas Polesie   Inga-Lill Johansson

Contents

Part 1

Assumptions about Rationality and Action

SOME REFLECTIONS ON HEDBERG & JÖNSSON'S SEMI-CONFUSING INFORMATION SYSTEMS 3

Jacob G. Birnberg
University of Pittsburgh

Part 2

The Scientific Enterprise

Part 3

Outlining Networks of Restrictions and Social Interaction

Part 4

Evolution of Corporate Policies

ACTION AND INTENTION
- Closure and Disclosure of Policies 133

Thomas Polesie
Gothenburg School of Economics and
Commercial Law

Part 5

Changes in Information Technology

CURRICULUM VITAE OF LUCA PACIOLI, 495 B SJ - 423 B SJ   203

Alf Sandin
Gothenburg School of Economics and Commercial Law

About the authors   211

Part 1

Assumptions about Rationality and Action

SOME REFLECTIONS ON HEDBERG & JÖNSSON'S SEMI-CONFUSING INFORMATION SYSTEMS

Jacob G. Birnberg
University of Pittsburgh

Abstract

Sten Jönsson's paper with Hedberg on semi-confusing information systems (1978) arguably is his best known work in the United States. Brown et. al. (1990) in their comprehensive review of citations to journal articles indicate that during the eleven years which they analyzed since the paper's publication there has been an average of 2.18 citations per year. This ranks quite high among managerial control oriented papers.

Given the significance of this paper in assessing Jönsson's reputation among English speaking behavioral accounting researchers, it is worthwhile to relate the "semi-confusing" paper to two other works that appeared at about the same time, i e Demski & Feltham (1978) and Ouchi (1979). Each paper has found a significant niche in the management control systems literature and each has a distinct focus and discusses different aspects of the planning and control process.

The intent of the paper is to compare and contrast these three papers to reflect how Jönsson's views are related to those of the other researchers. Like Ouchi and unlike Demski-Feltham, Jönsson takes a positive view of the actors' attitudes toward the Management Control System process. However, unlike Ouchi's clan oriented work, they place greater emphasis on the role of systems.

Introduction

The period from the late 1960s through the 1970s was, primarily, a renaissance period for financial accounting research. Driven by empirical work such as Ball and Brown (1968), the focus of financial accounting shifted from theory to data. What resulted was a significant imbalance in accounting research. A great deal of time and effort was devoted to researching financial accounting issues and relatively little to managerial control. However, during the late 1970s three papers appeared that would do for interest in research in managerial control what Ball and Brown (1968) did for financial accounting. These papers were Demski & Feltham (1978), Ouchi (1979) and Hedberg & Jönsson (1978). Each of these three papers made a significant contribution to our understanding of managerial control. Significantly, each discussed a different aspect of the managerial control process. As the result, comparing and contrasting these papers provides an interesting view of what different researchers think are the most important issues for the managerial control process.

The Three Papers

This section provides a brief summary of each paper. Its purpose is to highlight what the paper views to be the central issues in the managerial control problem and isolate some important assumptions.

Demski & Feltham

Demski & Feltham (1978) introduced agency theory as a model of the budget process and has served as a basis for an extensive literature in the area of managerial control. See Baiman (1982; 1990) for a review of the literature and an extended discussion of the theory.

Demski & Feltham view managerial control as the principal's problem: the desire of the principal to motivate the agent, so that the agent, while pursuing his or her self interest, simultaneously pursues the interests of the principal. This has been called "behavioral congruence" on the part of the agent.

This formulation of the problem suggests a totally businesslike relationship between the two parties. One where they contract over the agent's obligation (i e , decision making) and the principal's commitment to provide appropriate rewards (i e , incentives). Because this is a formal agreement, it must be drawn so that any dispute between the parties can be resolved by a third party. Thus the agreement focuses only on those data that can be verified, i e independently observed by an individual not a party to the agreement.

Both parties are economic persons. They behave in a rational, utility maximizing fashion. They possess unlimited computational powers. This includes the ability to assess the probability of events occurring and the ability to combine these assessments in a Bayesian manner. See Baiman (1982) for an extended discussion.

Figure 1, (adapted from Ouchi, 1979), reflects the basic problems facing the principal. It assumes adequate knowledge of the tranformation process exists. If the agent has a no more extensive data set than the principal and the critical aspects of any agreement are verifiable, we are in cell one and there is no problem for the principal. When a "cell one world" exists, the principal can offer the agent a series of contracts from which to choose. Principals will design the contracts so that they secure the best performance possible from agents given the work and risk averse characteristics of the typical agent.

Thus, in the cases of cells two and three the theory explains why the resulting contract between the two parties from the principal's perspective is less desirable than a cell one contract. (See Birnberg et. al. (1983) for a disccussion of what may happen if the principal fails to recognize or ignores the information asymmetry. Knowledge has been used in place of Ouchi's (1979) term of measurability because the ability to measure requires both knowledge of (1) what to measure and (2) a verifiable measurement. Since the principal-agent formulation assumes that only verifiable data are used in a contract the critical question is the principal's relative disadvantage over the set of verifiable knowledge, i e measurements.)

Observability of agent's acts

	High	Low
Knowledge		
High	1	2
of		
Low	3	4
Process		

Figure 1. Nature of Principal's Problem. Adapted from Ouchi (1979; Table 3).

The primary contribution of principal-agent analysis was to make explicit the formal structure of the problem facing the principal in both motivating and constraining the agent. This formalization both expanded the set of concepts discussed in the management control literatures, e g risk aversion, and formalized already existing concepts, e g, information asymmetries and incentives.

Those researchers who are less involved with the formal analysis usually focus on the highly restrictive assumptions of principal-agent analysis. One that draws particular attention is the assumption of unlimited rationality. A second is the assumption of complete self interest. Rejection of these assumptions leads to a discussion of the work of Ouchi and Theory Z.

Ouchi

Ouchi (1979) draws heavily on the transaction cost analysis view of the organization developed by Williamson (1975). The Williamson approach substitutes the concept of bounded rationality for unlimited rationality. As a result, both principals and agents are unable to use all they know to reach the best possible enforceable contract. In this approach either party may possess factual knowledge relevant to the problem, but be unable to recognize its relevance to the situation. Agents, faced with the employment contract offered by the principal, decide how they will behave so as to maximize their well being. They are involved in a game of sorts where the principal (manager) sets the rules (incentive scheme) and the agent (subordinate) then chooses the act most beneficial to the agent. Because the principals possess bounded rationality, they are unable to anticipate all the responses of their agents. The result can be behavior by the agents that has been labeled "gaming the performance indicator." These situations occur when the managers behave in ways that are consistent with the incentive scheme (rules) set by the manager, but not at all related to what the managers wanted or expected. A classic example includes managers at a nail factory who were evaluated by the weight of their output. Faced with the need to achieve the proper tonnage of production, they shifted from nails to spikes. The targeted production tonnage was achieved, but the mix of sizes and types did not conform to management's plan. This is the classic problem of the dysfunctional consequences of performance measurement identified much earlier by Ridgway (1956).

This exploitation of the incompleteness of the incentive contract by the agent results from Williamson's assumption that people act in their own self interest. Williamson labeled such behavior "opportunism" and he argued that the only way to minimize opportunistic behavior was through administrative rules. These rules result in added costs called "transaction costs."

Ouchi took the Williamson formulation in a different direction. He assumed that in some cultures and/or organizations self interest is not the dominate motive determining the behavior of the subordinates. Thus, he decided to analyze the same problem as Williamson had, but with an altered behavioral assumption. In Ouchi (1979) individuals made decisions that benefited the group; what Ouchi labeled the "clan". Thus, in his formulation of the management control problem Ouchi saw the central issue to be the need to achieve goal congruence among the organization's members either through selection, orientation, organizational environment or some mix of the three. The resulting individual could be labeled "clan man."

Ouchi could have analyzed all three of the cells which presented problems in the earlier principal-agent formulation. However, cells two and three present relatively trivial problems as Ouchi conceived of the world. His two dimensions, observability and knowledge/measurement, are absolutes. Only one needs to be present for the development of a viable control scheme. If the actions are observable but not measureable, i e , cell three, the control system will concentrate on the process. If the reverse is true and the outcome is measureable but the actions not observeable, i e , cell two, then outcome measures will be used for control. In Ouchi's world, all that is needed for a viable control system is one of the two possible dimensions to be present. This is true because clan members' goals are congruent with those of management and the control system is a way for the managers and the workers to identify and communicate to one another that congruent set of goals. A second way of looking at cells two and three is that the clan members would not exploit their asymmetry for their own advantage. Rather, they would inform management of any private information. This is in contrast with the behavioral assumptions of formal agency theory and Williamson's transaction cost analysis. (But see Baiman and Evans, 1983.) Thus, Ouchi's Theory Z is a theory intended to solve the problems found in cell 4 where the managers of the organization lack certain critical prerequisites for an effective Theory X or top down coordination system.

Ouchi's approach to control differs significantly from the formal principal-agent approach and suggests a totally different view of the process. The formal principal-agent approach relies on the task or situation's properties as well as the principal's and agent's characteristics to determine the nature of the control system required. However, Ouchi argues that by organizing and hiring according to certain predetermined patterns, the managers can affect the nature of the control problem they face. Management, rather than the task alone, affects the nature of the control system.

Moreover, the cell four world may reflect the control problem of the 1990s and early 21st century. Uncertainty is high and our ability to plan behaviors is much lower than it has been in earlier periods. The source of the uncertainty may be outside the organization rather than in the manager's or worker's understanding of the task. If this is true, then the uncertainty is less tractable by traditional control methods such as added and more detailed bureaucratic rules and procedures. However, Ouchi's view of the clan as a basis for organizational behavior and control does focus on a particular view of managerial style. However, the question remains whether all people can adopt such a view. (See Fucini & Fucini, 1990).

Hedberg & Jönsson

The work of Ouchi and Demski & Feltham raises three critical questions, but leaves them unanswered:

o   Why is there a lack of knowlege either in the absolute or in the relative?
o   How does the organization collect and disseminate the information it does have?
o   In the absence of a high level of knowledge, how do managers decide?

It is these questions that Hedberg & Jönsson attempt to answer in their landmark paper. In doing so they attempt to link the task structure (Demski & Feltham) and organization structure (Ouchi) to the information activities of the organization. Thus Hedberg & Jönsson's focus is on the role of information and information systems on managers' planning behavior. Their central theme is how to alter the managers' level of knowledge ("problem analyzability") and move from lower absolute knowledge level cells to higher absolute knowledge level cells. It is a dynamic theory because it discusses how managers shift from one (temporary) equilibrium to a new and better (temporary) equilibrium.

Turning to the 2x2 in Hedberg & Jönsson (figure 5;57) and the related discussion, it is apparent that problem variety affects the complexity of the manager's behavior but not the ability of a qualified manager to solve the present problem. Difficulty in resolving the problem is related to analyzability, a surrogate for absolute knowledge. Thus, the interesting questions to Hedberg & Jönsson are found in the unanalyzable condition and those analyzable task situations where the external change is not predictable. This yields a different 2x2 than the one discussed by Demski & Feltham and Ouchi. The relevant 2x2 is related entirely to how uncertainty affects the state of the manager's knowledge. One dimension is task related knowledge; what Hedberg & Jönsson call analyzability and what could be called "task related uncertainty." The second dimension relates to external or environmental change. This change is inherent in life. Very few environments are stable in the sense of never changing. However, some changes can be predicted with a higher degrees of accuracy and with greater lead times than others. Thus, the critical issue in the case of external change is whether the change in the external environment can be predicted early enough and with sufficient accuracy to be useful to managers.

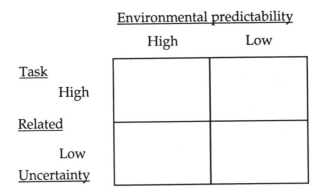

Figure 2. Sources of uncertainty in Hedberg & Jönsson

While cell one presents a trivial design problem, the other three cells require an information system that does more than provide passive, historical internal data. In the spirit of Argyris (1977) the role of the information system is to promote learning (i e understanding of the problem space) which is manifest in the dynamic aspects of organizational behavior. Learning results in both the abandoning of old standard operating procedures that are no longer deemed to be appropriate and the acquiring of new behaviors which, given the revised knowledge base, appear to be appriate.

To discuss such a problem, Hedberg & Jönsson must offer a more complex and wider ranging discussion of issues than Demski & Feltham and Ouchi do. Their paper draws on research ranging from cognitive psychology to sociology. Hedberg & Jönsson use the model of cognitive processes of Schroder et al. (1967) which also was used by early cognitive researchers in accounting, thereby associating their work with a significant segment of behavioral accounting research. At the same time, they focus on the role of myths and beliefs in organizations; an issue discussed by accounting researchers such as Hopwood, e g Burchell et al. (1978), and sociologists such as Thompson (1967). As will be noted in the next section, the result is a less tightly organized description of behavior than that offered by Ouchi and a less rigorous formal model than Demski & Feltham. However, it raises issues which should be of importance to managers and researchers. One indicator of this is the growing emphasis now found in the strategic planning literature on environmental intelligence. For example, see Prescott and Smith (1987).

If accounting researchers are to follow through on some of the provocative issues raised by Hedberg & Jönsson, they probably will be forced by the scope of the problem to decompose it and pursue segments of it. If this occurs, some of the richness found in the Hedberg & Jönsson formulation will be lost as richness is traded away to secure tractability and rigor.

Comparing and Contrasting the Papers

In this section the papers will be examined from two perspectives. The first examines the three papers from the perspective of a critical management control issue: How does the approach deal with dysfunctional subordinate behavior and its various potential causes? The second section takes a more comprehensive approach. That section

11

lists several critical dimensions of any approach to managerial information and control systems and compares the three papers on these
dimensions. This approach highlights the areas in which the papers
agree and, by implication, permits the reader to focus on those areas
where they differ.

Comparing and Contrasting on Dysfunctional Behavior

The papers may be compared using Venn style diagrams. See figure 3.
In figure 3a the circle labeled M represents the set of possible outcomes
desired by the managers. Because of its construction, it is not possible to
identify which point within M is Pareto superior to another point.
Similarly circle S represents the set of possible outcomes desired by
subordinates. In this case, too, there is no ordering within the circle.
Finally, circle C represents the set of outcomes that legally satisfy the
control system.

The numbers in each section of the diagram represent different
situations. Section 1 represents these outcomes valued by both parties
and permitted by the control system. Sections 2, 3, 5, and 6 represents
outcomes desired by only one party. Sections 3 and 5 are outside the
control system. Sections 6 represent outcomes permitted by the system
but desired only by management. Section 2 represents what often are
called dysfunctional consequences and in Williamson's formulation
result from the opportunistic behavior of the subordinate. Section 4
suggests that there are outcomes which both manager and subordinate
desire, but the existing control system does not legally permit. This
could be true either because it is not possible to design a control system
over these outcomes or because these outcomes are Pareto inferior for
both parties to those in section 1. Finally, section 7 represents outcomes
permitted but not desired by either party.

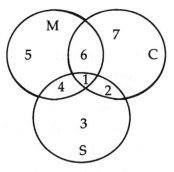

Figure 3(a) Traditional view of management control

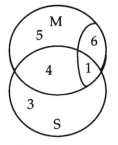

Figure 3(b) DF's formulation

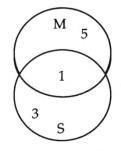

Figure 3(c) Ouchi's formulation

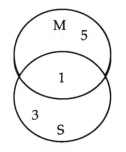

Figure 3(d) HJ's formulation

13

Demski & Feltham

Figures 3b, c and d apply this analysis to each of the papers. Figure 3b represents the Demski & Feltham/principal-agent formulation. While there may be many possible contracts, the theory argues that the manager will offer the contract(s) that will yield to him or her the best possible feasible outcome. Because of the manager's unbounded intellectual capacity, he will not offer a set of contract that does not contain at least one contract that is acceptable to both parties. The circle C has shrunk to a very small section of the diagram. The agent will select from section 1 and ignore section 6. The section labeled "2" in figure 3a no longer exists. Thus there is no basis for dysfunctional or opportunistic behavior in this formulation.

Ouchi

In contrast, figure 3c, which reflects Ouchi's cell four, does not have a control system in the traditional sense (figure 3a) or in the contractual sense (figure 3b). Rather activities which take place prior to the operating period align the goals or values of the subordinates with those of the managers. Ouchi specifies no formal mechanism to insure that the outcome selected within the intersection is the best for the organization. Rather, he relies on the Durkheimian notion of equity norms. The closer management has come in achieving a clan, the more greater the intersection of M and S and the more likely it is that the subordinates will achieve the outcome most valued by the organization.

Hedberg & Jönsson

Figure 3d represents Hedberg & Jönsson's work. In the discussion there is no overt concern with control. However, since some form of evaluation system is likely to exist, the question is the extent to which the ideal information system reinforces managers' pursuit of the goals of organization. One interpretation of the absense of a discussion of control is that Hedberg & Jönsson considered the firm to be similar to Ouchi's clan. In that case the control circle is omitted and the object of Hedberg & Jönsson's proposal is to improve the information system so that circle S is more consistent with the circle M. Consistency in this case refers to increasing outcomes valued by the organization and eliminating those which should not be. The arrows reflect the dynamic nature of the Hedberg & Jönsson formulation.

A second justification for the omission of the control circle, C, is the strategic orientation of Hedberg & Jönsson's task. At the strategic level control is less formal and often geared to a very broad set of criteria. Many of these criteria are qualitative and process oriented rather than quantitative and outcome measurement oriented. Indeed, Hedberg & Jönsson's emphasis on the dynamic nature of the process suggests that they are discussing either a situation found in Ouchi's cell four where he advocates the clan or, at best, a situation where we have limited insight into the process the managers should have undertaken. In the latter case, what the superior knows only imperfectly is how his subordinate(s) should attempt to resolve the problem. The superior does not know what the manager should do nor exactly what should be measured. Thus the control system, circle C, is not (or at least should not be) articulated with the same degree of detail as in either Demski & Feltham or the traditional view of a control system. It could be represented, perhaps, by a circle whose outline is dotted to reflect its ambiguous and often ex post nature.

Summary

Reviewing the three figures, one is struck by the differences they mirror in the papers. Demski & Feltham is a "traditional" view of managerial control augmented by the assumed high level of knowledge and self interest that aspired to what could be called a "cell one world," one where no intractable problems exist. While all situations may not lead to first best solutions, the goal is the elimination of dysfunctional and opportunistic behavior. Agency researchers relax particular assumptions and make others, e g, agents are risk averse not risk neutral, in their pursuit of this goal. Thus, in any given setting, Demski & Feltham present a method for resolving management's, i e the principal's, control problem.

In contrast, Ouchi offers insight into how the same organizational objectives can be attained without the strong knowledge assumption if one is willing to relax the self interest assumption. This view reflected the search by managers and theorists for an explanation for the patterns of management found in Japanese firms. See Birnberg and Snodgrass (1988). Thus, the two approaches suggests that different situations respond better to different philosophies of managerial control. What they do not resolve is whether or not the setting dictates the style or whether the manager/organization determines the style.

Finally, Hedberg & Jönsson, like Ouchi, accept the inherent difficulty in establishing formal systems. They argue that, when the environment is dynamic and/or not well understood, investing heavily in a formal information and control system may be the wrong thing to do. A significant investment of monetary and/or human resources can result in a reluctance to consider the need for change. Instead, managers facing uncertain situations should consider "disposable" systems. Systems that are relatively inexpensive to design, can be put in place quickly and present relatively few problems of "negative transfer" (The ability of the user to shift from the old system to the new system is not inhibited by prior use of the old system.). In this regard the domain investigated by Hedberg & Jönsson is similar to that investigated by Ouchi. However, they investigate behavior in that particular cell in far greater detail than did Ouchi.

Comparison on Various Dimensions

In this section a more detailed comparison of the papers is undertaken. The various dimensions are shown in Table 1. For a similar approach but not to these papers, per se, see Eisenhardt (1988). In this paper four aspects of the control process are examined- the orientation, view of people, task and the implications.

Orientation

Much of the previous material has been devoted to analyzing the orientation of each paper and comparing and contrasting the papers. See, for example, the previous sections. Thus, this section of Table 1 serves to synthesize much of the earlier discussion.

16

Table 1. Comparing the three papers

	Demski-Feltham	Ouchi	Hedberg-Jönsson
1. Orientation			
a. Intent of MCS	Efficient use of principal's resources	Deal with uncertainty through clan behaviors through MIS	Deal with uncertainty
b. Portion of MCS (by incentive)	Motivate (by values)	Motivate (Data Set)	Deciding
c. Responsibility Level of agent	Operation or decentralized manager	Operating team (operations & managing)	Managerial and strategic
d. Role of Incentives	Behavioral congruence	Reinforce clan values	Not discussed
2. View of People	Economic man	Clan man	Administrative man
3. View of Task			
a. Relevance of Task	Characteristics determine incentive contract	Only certain tasks considered	Defines information system problem
b. Level of Information	Varies with situation	Low	Varies with situation
c. Information Asymmetry	Always present in some form	High	Not considered
d. Form of uncertainty	Problem-structured; Data-Probability distribution (Risk)	Ill-structured problem	Changing problem, so it varies
4. Implications			
a. Dysfunctional behavior	Minimized by proper contract	Minimized by clan values	Minimized by information system design
b. Learning	By principal regarding agent's information	By clan members concerning task	By managers concerning their environment

View of People

The descriptors in this category reflect the philosophical differences inherent in the three papers and their view of the management process. Obviously, how you approach a non-trivial situation depends upon the nature of the people as well as the task. Two of the three papers take extreme views. Ouchi's clan man would score very high on dimensions such as the importance of the group relative to the individual, desirability of cooperation, avoidance of conflict, conformity to group norms and loyalty to the group In contrast, economic man would place the greatest importance on self interest, personal rewards and would reject the role of group norms, per se, unless their violation had legal and/or economic costs.

In contrast to these two stereotypes, administrative man as viewed by Hedberg & Jönsson is intellectually fallible and systems must be designed to facilitate his understanding. Not only is administrative man's intellectual adaptivity limited, so is his ability to ascertain when change has occurred. Again, it is the role of systems to assist this manager.

The contrast is a simple one. In the case of clan man and economic man their strengths mean that the system should be designed to support them. However, in the case of administrative man the system is intended to make the manager more effective by improving his decision making ability. Thus the system is intended to help by supporting administrative man where he is limited and utilize the strengths of economic and clan man.

Task

While Table 1 lists four subdimensions under task, the most important aspect and the one which summarizes the papers' divergent views is the "form of uncertainty." Demski & Feltham's economic man is a decision maker and decisions require both models and data. Thus Demski & Feltham view the available data as being expressable by probability distributions at the very worst. This means that those data available to the managers are expressed in a form which a Bayesian manager and subordinate can process. That the available data are "that good" should come as no surprise.

Ouchi's managers view their primary task as working together to enhance their performance. Like Demski & Feltham's economic man, they are decision makers. However, the problem is not deciding among alternatives, but rather one of ascertaining as best they can the structure of the problem. Once the problem has been structured, the decision, in a relative sense, is easy. Thus, Ouchi suggests that in some cases problem definition not problem solving is the issue.

Similarly, Hedberg & Jönsson's managers also are interested in structuring the problem. However, Hedberg & Jönsson argue that, because of external uncertainty, we need systems to be sure that we are structuring and/or solving the _right_ problem. Given a high degree of external uncertainty, Ouchi's managers could resolve the wrong problem. Hedberg & Jönsson are trying to provide their managers with cues that will avoid this problem.

Thus, the three papers offer a progression of task difficulty. In part, the contrast between Demski & Feltham on the one hand and Ouchi and Hedberg & Jönsson on the other reflects the cognitive skills of the manager. Economic man, by definition, knows what he needs to know. However, the data may not be available. In the case of clan man and administrative man it is not necessarily true that the data requirements are known. Defining that set is part of the manager's task.

Summary and Conclusions

Section four of Table 1 represents a summary of what has been discussed thus far. It reflects that all the papers in their own ways are interested in developing more efficient and effective control systems. The key to how this will occur is through changes in the behavior of the parties as they acquire new data bases or alter existing data structures or even ascertain entirely new problem situations. These changes re–present learning by one or both of the parties to the control system.

Who learns, how they learn and why they learn have been discussed in this paper. It is these differences that provide insight into the substantive differences among the papers in this regard. And as noted earlier, the work of Hedberg & Jönsson provides a dynamic view of the decision maker's problem.

References

Argyris, C., (1977), Organizational Learning and M.I.S., <u>Accounting, Organizations and Society</u>, 2, pp 113-124.

Baiman, S., (1982), Agency Research in Management Accounting: A Survey, <u>Journal of Accounting Literature</u>, pp 155-173.

Baiman, S., (1990), Agency Research in Management Accounting: A Second Look, <u>Accounting, Organizations and Society</u>, 4 pp 341-372.

Baiman, S., Evans, J. H., (1983), Pre-Decision Information and Participative Management Control Systems, <u>Journal of Accounting Research</u>, Spring, pp 371-395.

Ball, W., Brown, P, (1972), An Empiricial Evaluation of Accounting Income Numbers, <u>Journal of Accounting Research</u> , Autumn, pp 159- 178.

Birnberg, J., Snodgrass, C., (1988), Culture and Control: A Field Study, <u>Accounting, Organizations and Society</u>, 5, pp 447-464.

Birnberg, J., Turopolec, L., Young, S. M., (1983), The Organizational Context of Accounting, <u>Accounting, Organizations and Society</u>, 2/3, pp 111-129.

Brown, L., Gardner, J., Vasarhelyi, M., (1989), Accounting Research Directory, New York: Weiner.

Burchell, S., Clubb, C., Hopwood, A., Hughes, J., Nahapiet, J., (1979), The Roles of Accounting in Organizations, Accounting, Organizations and Society, 1 pp 5-30.

Demski, J., Feltham, G., (1978), Economic Incentives in Budgetary Systems, Journal of Accounting Research, April, pp 336-358.

Esienhardt, K., (1988), Agency and Institutional Theory Explanations: The Case of Retail Sales Compensation, Academy of Management Journal, 3, pp 488-511.

Fucini, J., Fucini, S., (1990), Working for the Japanese: Inside Mazda's American Auto Plant, New York: Free Press.

Hedberg, B., Jönsson, S., (1978), Designing Semi-Confusing Information Systems for Organizations in Changing Environments, Accounting, Organizations and Society, 1, pp 47- 64.

Ouchi, W., (1979), A Conceptual Framework for the Design of Organizational Control Mechanisms, Management Science, September, pp 833-848.

Prescott, J., Smith, D., (1987), A Project-Based Approach to Competitive Analyses, Strategic Management Journal, pp 411-423.

Ridgway, V., (1956), Dysfunctional Consequences of Performance Measurement, Administrative Science Quarterly, September, pp 240-247.

Schroder, H., Driver, M., Streufert, M., (1967), Human Information Processing, New York: Holt.

Thompson, J., (1967), Organizations in Action, New York: McGraw-Hill.

Williamson, O., (1975), Markets and Hierarchies: Analysis and Antitrust Implications, NewYork: Free Press.

ACCOUNTING AND TRUST:
Some Implications for Management Control

Mahmoud Ezzamel
Hugh Willmott
University of Manchester
Institute of Science and Technology

Introduction

Trust has received considerable attention from researchers in economics (e g Arrow, 1974; Hirshman, 1984; Dasgupta, 1988; Lorenz, 1988), sociologists (e g Garfinkel, 1963; Zand, 1972; Fox, 1974; Luhmann, 1979; 1988; Hawthorn, 1988), organisation theorists (e g Pollard, 1965; Wildavsky, 1975; March and Olsen, 1976; Mintzberg, 1983) and psychologists (e g Good, 1988). Yet, surprisingly, only very few accounting researchers have focused explicitly on trust (Jönsson 1990; Armstrong, 1991; Neu, 1991; Ezzamel, 1991).

Despite the paucity of research in accounting that focuses explicitly on trust, the notion of trust underlies a significant body of accounting research, particularly that which is attentive to the behavioural dimension. For example, much of the literature on participation in budget setting is implicitly rooted in trust relations; superiors' trust in subordinates not deliberately falsifying their targets, and subordinates' trust in superiors taking their budget submissions seriously (e g Argyris, 1953; Becker and Green, 1962; Hughes, 1965). Even in the non-behavioural literature, trust relations are often implicitly assumed. For example, in the context of determining transfer prices for intra-company products, it is typically assumed that division managers act in good faith when submitting supply and demand schedules (e g Hirshleifer, 1956; Samuels, 1969). Similarly, reward schemes, such as that of Groves (1973), are presumed to engender truthful submission of information. Trust relations thus permeate much of the activity exposed in the 'conventional' management accounting literature.

Despite the usefulness of this literature and its immediate relevance to the understanding of trust, it suffers from three main limitations. Firstly, it studies trust in an implicit manner thereby failing to bring it to the fore of analysis. Second, and relatedly, it fails to address the dynamics of trust relations; how they unfold and change, and how they influence organisational processes and participants. Thirdly, the implicit conception of trust has tended to be quite narrow, focusing in the main on honesty and truthfulness of individuals whilst ignoring the institutional structures which promote or undermine assessment of the relations of trust (see Fox, 1974).

Two recent studies (Jönsson and Grönlund, 1988; Johnson, 1990) break new ground in accounting research by examining the dynamics of trust relations in some detail. In particular, the 1990 paper explores the relationship between trust relations and organisational performance by linking investment in trust (symbolic capital) to greater economic efficiency. This chapter presents a review and evaluation of this work. The next section summarises Jönsson's theoretical framework in which he links trust and the need for improvement in accounting. The third section summarises the main contributions of Jönsson's study to our understanding of trust. The fourth section seeks to extend the discussion of trust by arguing that the question of economic efficiency cannot be sensibly divorced from that of moral acceptability - as Jönsson's work itself reveals. Hence, our discussion considers the extent to which the mobilisation of trust for purposes of economic efficiency is constrained as well as enabled by the moral-political organisation of the relations in which trust is defined and 'won'. The final section contains a summary of the paper.

Need for Improvement and Trust

Like many academic accountants during the last decade, Jönsson has been concerned with developing recipes for improving the relevance and utility of management accounting to its users. He associates relevance of information directly to "the uniqueness of the situation in which the information is used". In order to reclaim lost relevance he argues "the user should be provided with support in relating the accounting data to the activities under his control". In the cases examined in 'Accounting for Improvement' this support takes the form of a transformation of front line operational units into 'centres of trust'.

Jönsson draws on Morgan (1986) to characterise the design philosophy of traditional management accounting systems as "machine-like", vested with intentions, calculations, and rationality. This may be appropriate in a stable world. However, environmental turbulence exposes the inadequacies of this philosophy as it becomes evident that organisational survival can be engineered only through shifting the design philosophy from the "machine" metaphor to the "organic" metaphor. Under the latter, some measure of decentralisation is necessary as strategic and control information become not only centrally but also locally located.

Jönsson considers two alternative solutions to the above problem: either a 'top-down' redesign of management accounting systems or a 'bottom-up' design of local systems to deal competently with environmental challenges. He opts for the latter alternative on the basis of immediacy to the causes which lead to the 'loss of relevance'. Much of that 'loss of relevance', he argues, occurs at the local management level where control is immediate, processual, ad hoc, unique, concrete and causal, in contrast to central control which tends to be abstract, standardised and goal and output oriented (see also Argyris, 1977). In order to reclaim relevance accounting systems must provide "supporting local systems that re-establish the link between activity logic and the control logic of the firm".

To conceptualise the distinctive features of the activity of 'front line' units, in which accounting has most relevance for 'ad hoc' model building in search for solutions to operational problems, Jönsson draws on the work of institutional theorists such as Meyer and Scott (1983) and Brunsson (1989) but more particularly Bourdieu (1977). Specific environmental configurations are understood to lead to the emergence of <u>habitus</u>, or socially constituted systems or entities, whose dispositions lead to the generation and structuration of what may be interpreted as regular, but <u>not mechanistic</u> practices. Hence, each entity constitutes itself and its members are held together by a social bond manifested in a prevailing ethos which defines "acceptable" and "unacceptable" conduct for them. This ethos is the product of a learning process which is impacted upon by task structure and by other forms of regularity.

Upon being constituted, each entity (e g operational units) engages in contractual interactions with other entities. Trust, conceptualised by Jönsson as symbolic capital in terms of honour and prestige, is generated as the ultimate and inevitable outcome of the successful forging and execution of contracts between entities, which require symbolic investment in terms of both resources and time. The entity's access to environmental (external) resources is enhanced as its stock of trust appreciates. Intra-unit contracts are typically implicit (revealed in behaviour) and their maintenance requires time, i e is costly, while inter-unit contracts are explicit (revealed in accounts). But the argument rests ultimately on the costs and benefits calculus for the investment in trust, and hence a central question is "whether the investment in symbolic capital occurs at the expense of economic efficiency and what organisational conditions may enhance complementarity rather than conflict between the accumulation of symbolic and economic capital".

Jönsson's Field Studies

Considering two field sites - automated production in Volvo and a number of caring institutions - Jönsson utilises the above framework to show how 'trust' relationships can be promoted and then mobilised, to productive effect.

In the Volvo plant which produced parts (e g brake drums for heavy vehicles) the local management team, comprising a foreman and members of two production lines, were granted 'extended authority and self-management'. Decision-making at the plant level became more highly participative with local actors being made responsible for diagnosing problems, collecting information perceived to be relevant to each problem, and, on the basis of this information, dealing with the problem and maintaining appropriate information feedback. Attention was focused upon the temporary need for information at local levels thereby obviating the need for centralised reporting and storing of information which is relevant only occasionally. The confidence engendered by this discretion was found to encourage local groups to share their work experiences and to resolve problems of inter-dependence through direct communications with other groups such as the unit responsible for sand blasting blank brake drums.

The incentive scheme agreed between the plant and top management demonstrated how payment systems can be refined to accommodate and reinforce self-management. Salaries were renegotiated every six months, and these reflected a negotiated production rate. If actual results exceeded those initially negotiated, the company recouped all the benefits but employees stood a good chance to negotiate a higher salary during the next period. Conversely, when actual output was below the level reflected in the agreed salaries, no salary reductions were imposed by top management during that period but employees were in a weaker negotiating position in the next period. As Jönsson comments: "In this way the group has a good reason to maintain the trust of the company and the contract relation is kept visible".

These relationships produced a substantial economic reward. Over a four year period, productivity progressively increased from 2.1% to 13.2% and staff turnover was reduced dramatically. Thus, in the case of the Volvo plant, investment in symbolic capital was consistent with the enhancement of economic efficiency.

Jönsson's other case study concerned the use of accounting in municipal caring organisations. There, investment in symbolic capital took the form of accounting training and dialogue through direct contacts between the local responsibility centres and the central controller's department. Also, a decentralised system was in operation. The tailoring of accounting systems to local needs was embedded in informed discretion and dialogue, and these attributes were highly valued by the members of responsibility centres. Local managers were allowed to make their own calculations with respect to a wide range of local activities. This in turn contributed to a reduction in perceived uncertainty and enhanced the ability of local managers to form more comprehensive and accurate views of the economic environment.

Through the exchange of ideas between local managers and the controller's department, problems were diagnosed and solutions were suggested which resulted in improved service flow and quality. Also, the use of dialogues was "conducive to the emergence of projects out of ideas that would under normal conditions remain discursive". Again, as in the case of the Volvo plant, investment in symbolic capital was conducive to increased economic efficiency: the economic benefits of writing and executing contracts exceeded the costs.

These two field studies both complement and reinforce each other. In both studies, the driving force behind rational decision-making and economic efficiency was the increased level of control gained by responsibility centre managers over their local environments. In both studies the twin vehicles for increased local controllability were informal dialogues (e g team briefing) and responsible contracting - that is, attaining 'an agreement of mutual action between consenting parties'. In a trust environment, time spent on dialogues and direct contacts with other local and central managers was no longer perceived by local managers as being wasteful, or as a misappropriation of time away from their core activities. Rather, it was perceived as time well spent since it resulted in time savings elsewhere. But the richness of the findings does not stop there; additional insights are gained from the diversity of the two field study sites.

In the production setting of the Volvo plant, where the dialogue was internal to the local group, it created a basis for contracting with other local groups to manage interdependence. This internal focus, Jönsson argues, may be explained by the prevalence of the Taylorist tradition of fragmented tasks in production settings, thereby rendering internal dialogues necessary. In the caring sites, the dialogue was located at the local unit/central controllers department interface. This, Jönsson ar-gues, is consistent with the nature of the caring service as the focus is usually on interaction with clients. Continued economic improvements achieved by local units was therefore attained through improved knowledge of local conditions, and this reinforced trust relationships as knowledgeable local managers became more increasingly trusted by more senior managers as partners in the control dialogue.

Discussion

Jönsson's case studies illustrate two basic points about accounting systems. Firstly, that they are widely used to produce information for use by central/senior management rather than local/supervisory levels of management. Secondly, that making them relevant for local management requires the co-operation of lower managerial levels - the foreman and operatives at Volvo, the managers of the caring establishments in the municipal study. These two points are not un-connected. Accounting data for senior management are not generated simply to provide them with information, in statistical form, about operational activity. Rather, their purpose is to render the productivity of labour more visible to senior management, and to provide a basis for intervention and <u>control</u>. Centralised, top-down accounting systems are developed not just to support strategic decision-making but also, and more fundamentally, to support a framework of <u>discipline</u> which secures a minimal level of co-operation.

The (bureaucratic) framework of discipline is needed precisely because the spontaneous co-operation of employees in meeting the objectives of their employer cannot be taken for granted. In principle, there would be little need for centralised accounting control systems if employees shared the objectives of their employer (e g lower unit-costs), and sought unreservedly to define their activities so as to achieve these objectives. However, in practice, this ideal (from the perspective of management) is rarely fulfilled because the contractual nature of the relationship between employer and employee is fundamentally instru-mental, not moral. The nature of this relationship means that the employer is more interested in reducing the cost of labour and raising its productivity; and for the employee the priorities are reversed. In the context of a <u>capitalist</u> employment relationship - such as the one at

Volvo the concern to raise productivity is heightened by the demands of shareholders to secure an adequate rate of return on their investment.

The design and development of centralised accounting systems can be seen as a means of surveillance, developed by senior management, to monitor and control unit-costs, including the cost of labour. However, as Jönsson's case studies usefully demonstrate, the very presence and operation of these accounting systems can have unintended consequences. Specifically, they contribute to the creation or reinforcement of a situation in which employees are, in effect, prevented from taking day-to-day responsibility for their activity. Prior to the introduction of the 'self management' programmes, staff had been deprived of the resources - both material (e g Personal Computers and incentive payments) and ideological ('trust' in operative staff) - which subsequently were considered necessary for them to address operational problems and concerns.

This deprivation was not accidental. For Taylorist and Fordist philosophies of work design are founded upon the understanding that efficient manufacture depends upon the systematic divorce of conception (management) from execution (productive activity). The rationale which underpins this philosophy is that delegation of authority to workers (self-management) increases their capacity to resist and disrupt the most efficient systems of manufacture. The expansion of the 'symbolic capital' of labour is based upon the calculation that a tightly regulated form of "workers' control" offers a more direct and effective method of reducing wastage and improving quality.

When evaluating this reform, it is necessary to appreciate how the strategy of fostering trust relations is embedded within a wider institutional structure of capital-labour relations. Within this structure the fate of trust is governed by rationalistic cost-benefit analysis. Forms and levels of trust are tied to this economic calculus rather than being valued as an integral element of organisational relations or culture. This commodification of trust is highly restrictive not only because the cost-benefit calculus is an imperfect art but also because it strips the concept of trust down to its most mechanistic and instrumental dimensions.

This argument can be developed by considering Dasgupta's (1983) attempt to invoke rationalistic economic reasoning in the analysis of trust. A central theme in his work is that trust relations are premised on the availability of a credible enforcement agency which has access to a suitable incentive machinery and which can impose suitable punishment on actors who behave opportunistically. Furthermore, any conception of trust as a meaningful value (ends) rather than as a lubricant (means) of control is denied. Just like any other economic commodity, trust is subjected to the costs and benefits calculus (Dasgupta, 1988, p 54):

"If the incentives are 'right', even a trustworthy person can be relied upon to be untrustworthy. 'Every man has his price': repugnant though it is to our sensibilities, the cliché captures the view that no one awards an infinite weight to his own honesty".

Hence, in the economic tradition every 'rational' actor is assumed to work out, or behave as if s/he works out, a matrix detailing the pay-offs associated with high trust, low trust and no-trust strategies and then to treat as the cost of commitment to trust 'the price that has to be paid for each party to trust the others to fulfil the terms of the agreement'. In economistic analysis, trust relations are seen merely as an alternative form of economic contracting; one which minimises transactions costs under a given set of specific conditions because comprehensive contracting is either impossible or forbiddingly costly. Such situations in which trust would be deemed economically expedient include instances of dependence between contracting parties which may be caused by them being locked into investments in specific assets or because they operate in the face of discontinuity and uncertainty (Lorenz, 1988).

Such restrictive assumptions are reinforced further as Dasgupta goes on to assume that the decision by actors to invest in building their own 'reputation' as trustworthy hangs precariously upon whether or not the economic benefits to them of creating the 'aura' of honest behaviour exceeds those of dishonest behaviour. Indeed, it is further assumed that when investing in 'reputation', actors typically restrict the level of their investment to the level of benefits they draw from trust; benefits to other actors and to society have to be paid for by those others, and hence 'there might be typically an under-investment in trust formation'.

We have focused on Dasgupta's work as an example of the economistic treatment of trust because many of its limitations are germane to the framework used by Jönsson. Taken to its natural conclusion, and given its restrictive assumptions, the analysis implies that it becomes exceedingly difficult, if not impossible, for trustworthy actors to distinguish themselves clearly from untrustworthy actors since distinguishing signals are either too costly or can be readily imitated. But this abstracts away from inter-personal and institutional relationships which inevitably construct, sustain and impede the social organisation of trust relations. Rooting trust relations exclusively in the web of economic rationality reduces seriously their scope and ethos compared with social relations. As Fox (1974), following Blau (1964), has pointed out, social 'exchange' necessarily involves <u>unspecified</u> obligations. Social relations always involve a 'moral' element, however limited and distorted it may be. Economistic conceptions of exchange represent transactions as if they are effectively regulated by contracts alone which stipulate the quantities to be exchanged. They fail to appreciate how exchange involves 'understandings' between actors which create <u>diffuse</u> future expectations (Garfinkel, 1967). And, in doing so, they naturalise and reinforce a historically specific tendency, promoted in capitalist society, to deny the irremediably moral quality of social reality by reducing relationships to a cash nexus in which all values and virtues take on the appearance of exchangeable commodities.

It is precisely because neo-classical economics is adopted as a calculus for disciplining work organisation that models which invoke economic rationality are of (limited) assistance in explaining organisational practices. For example, they may enable us to understand why trust relations are favoured in some organisations but not in others; or why they are promoted within some work groups but not amongst others (Friedman, 1977). They may be of assistance in understanding why the levels of trust relations can fluctuate dramatically over time in the same organisation. This latter question is of particular relevance to Jönsson's field studies for one is inclined to ask why, given a history of denying autonomy to operative staff, senior management became interested in expanding the autonomy of the staff in operational units. Arguably, the enthusiasm for delegation and decentralisation was more a product of economic necessity than any moral concern to establish and maintain genuinely trusting relationships. At Volvo, it was only when senior management complained about the ineffectiveness of the existing system for 'the management of operations' - a euphemism for the productivity of the workforce - that experimentation with a local system was sanctioned. Similarly, in the municipality interest in decentralised accounting systems was sparked and legitimised by 'debate on the productivity of the public sector'.

In each research site, senior management was obliged to acknowledge their fundamental dependence upon the co-operation of lower level employees for improvements in productivity. Interest in 'self management' was inspired by the realisation that centralised accounting systems simply did not provide information that was sufficiently timely or relevant for reducing overhead costs. In the past, this dependence had been obscured by the idea that control could be secured by restricting, if not wholly eliminating, the autonomy of those working in operational units. Accordingly, senior management developed and institutionalised forms of control - including the centralised accounting system - on the assumption that the key to productivity improvement lay in removing from the operational level opportunities to disrupt or deviate from the procedures laid down from above. However, this denial of discretion meant that there was little or no scope for staff to make adjustments and changes that would increase productivity. In short, existing forms of control such as the centralised accounting system reflected and reinforced an exchange relationship of institutionalised low trust in which, according to Fox (1974 : 73), there is:

'(a) a perceived disposition on the part of superordinates to behave as if the role occupant cannot be trusted, of his own volition, to perform according to their goals and values; (b) the imposition, as a conse-quence, of....specific impersonal rules, or other forms of systematic control; (c) the imposition, too, of tight co-ordination through exter-nally applied standardised routines and schedules, thereby ruling out the unrestricted communication and interaction patterns more appro-priate for certain kinds of problem solving...'

We have noted how Jönsson characterises the changes at his two research sites in terms of the creation of 'centres of trust' in which operational units become 'trusted responsible partners' as a 'dialogue' develops between themselves and higher, central levels. However, without denying that giving greater autonomy to operational units involves what may be termed 'trust', it is perhaps necessary to sound a note of scepticism concerning the extent to which 'trust' adequately describes a situation in which the autonomy of operational staff is limited and compromised by the institutional conditions in which it is extended.

Earlier, when reflecting upon the introduction of limited 'self-management', we observed that the 'trust' placed in members of the operational units described in the case studies was highly conditional. In particular, it was dependent upon achieving results that are acceptable to senior management. That a low-trust relationship underlies the apparently 'trusting' attitude of Volvo senior management is perhaps most evident in the extent to which changes in operations are directly related to payments triggered by (immediate) productivity improvements. The use of incentives suggests that management did not 'trust' the workforce spontaneously to exercise their autonomy to raise productivity. Paradoxically, the very design of the system of 'self management' confirmed that 'trust' had to be bought.

With regard to the Volvo case at least, there is a danger that use of the term 'trust' obscures what amounted to a bargain struck between central and operational management in which senior managers bought the willingness of operational staff to co-operate in the development of a system that raised their productivity. Equally, there is a danger of reducing the benefits to Volvo operational staff to an increase in their wages that followed from their co-operation in raising productivity. As Jönsson notes, work relations involve issues of identity as well as material self-interests. If, as would be expected, the established system of centralised control generated resentment and unwillingness to co-operate amongst some staff (because it denied them opportunities to express and confirm their self-understanding as autonomous, responsible adults), it is likely the new system was more acceptable and attractive to them. In this respect, it is possible - indeed, it is likely - that self-management at the operational level improved employee commitment and provided a basis for a subsequent expansion of a tightly regulated form of autonomy.

Running through Jönsson's discussion of 'Accounting for Improvement' is the idea that trust is something which subordinates within organisational hierarchies can earn by fulfilling the requirements of their superiors. In our view, this is a deeply managerial and potentially totalitarian usage of the concept of trust. In effect, trust is defined as obedience to those in authority. The trustworthiness of operative units is assessed in terms of their willingness to comply with the demands of senior management. 'Trust', which Jönsson rightly notes is associated with prestige and honour, is deployed by management as a means of recognising and rewarding compliant behaviour. 'Trust', in the form of greater autonomy and discretion, is bestowed only so long as this autonomy is exercised in ways which are judged acceptable by another. In practice, autonomy turns out to be heteronomy.

Institutionally, the members of operational units are rewarded - by learning to secure the trust of management - for relating to the centre as a colony relates to an imperial power. They are 'free' to act so long as these actions are shown to be productive in terms of criteria determined by the centre. They are 'trusted' only so long as they are compliant. A positive (i e managerially acceptable) response to an initial increase in autonomy raised the symbolic capital (honour and prestige) of operational management in the eyes of central management, with the consequence that central management has greater confidence in the 'trustworthiness' of the lower levels to which decision-making had been delegated. Underlying an expressed concern to create 'centres of trust' and greater 'dialogue' is an effort to sustain the existing institutional order. Concealed by the invitation to slip on the velvet glove is the priority of preserving the iron fist.

It is here that the wider social and political significance of Jönsson's studies becomes apparent. In common with other moves towards more 'participative' forms of management -- including 'team briefings', 'quality circles', 'interactive' accounting systems, etc - efforts to establish 'local management control' can be interpreted as efforts to raise productivity by disciplining employee subjectivity (Knights and

Willmott, 1989). As Jönsson notes, such programmes differ from the classical, Taylorian treatment of supervisory management and operational staff as mere objects of control who are required to perform tasks determined by others. Increased 'participation', linked to the incentive of productivity bonuses, provides a powerful means of 'educating' workers into managerial values or, at least, of gaining their 'consent' to the pursuit of objectives determined by senior management (Burawoy, 1979). Whereas untutored or union-guided reflection upon their situation might have led operational staff to question the legitimacy of the institutional structure or the ethics of management's interest in building 'trust', the effect of participating in the programme of 'self management', led by their foreman, was to promote a more self-disciplined orientation to work in which managerial definitions of what is problematic about work - set up times, quality, maintenance - dominate their 'dialogues'. As noted earlier, this focusing of their attention may be welcomed not simply because it is linked to pay increases but also, and perhaps more importantly, because it is crucial for building or confirming a conception of self as autonomous and responsible.

Conclusion

As Jönsson notes when concluding his paper, it is dangerous to generalise on the basis of two cases. Echoing this sentiment, we acknowledge our commentary has suggested the need to situate studies of 'local' accounting systems in their wide historical and institutional context. This has led us to explore tensions within programmes designed to establish 'centres of trust' within contexts of institutionalised low trust. If analysis of the wider institutional setting is ignored, there is a danger that managerial conceptions of 'trust' are uncritically accepted and the significance of contradictory forces within 'trust relations' remains unexamined. Consideration of the background of an employment relationship based upon institutionalised low trust suggests that however well meaning in intent, 'trust building' programmes are fundamentally manipulative. For this reason, they are readily compromised or abandoned if other measures - such as a programme of redundancies or short-time working are deemed more effective in controlling unit-costs. In welcoming studies which address the relevance of accounting for programmes of improvement, we believe that research into programmes must take greater account of the institutional contexts in which its 'relevance' is defined and pursued.

References

Argyris, C., (1953), Human Problems with Budgets, <u>Harvard Business Review</u>, Vol 31 (1), January-February, pp 97-110.

Armstrong, P., (1991), Contradiction and Social Dynamics in the Capitalist Agency Relationship, <u>Accounting, Organizations and Society</u> (forthcoming).

Arrow, K.J., (1974), The Limits of Organization, New York: Noston & Company.

Becker, S. and Green, D. Jr, (1962), Budgeting and Employee Behavior, <u>Journal of Business</u>, Vol 34 (4), pp 392-402.

Blau, P., (1964), Exchange and Power in Social Life, New York: Wiley & Sons.

Brunsson, N., (1991), The Organization of Hypocrisy, Chichester: Wiley & Sons.

Bourdieu, P., (1977), Outline of A Theory of Practice, Cambridge: Cambridge University Press.

Burawoy, M., (1979), Manufacturing Consent, University of Chicago Press.

Dasgupta, P., (1988), Trust as a Commodity, in D. Gambetta (ed), Trust: Making and Breaking Co-operative Relations, Oxford: Blackwell, pp 49-72.

Ezzamel, M., (1991), Incremental and Comprehensive Budgeting: Implications of Power and Organisational Change, University of Manchester Institute of Science and Technology Working Paper.

Fox, A., (1974), Beyond Contract: Work, Power and Trust Relations, London: Faber and Faber.

Friedman, A., (1977), Industry and Labour: Class Struggle at Work and Monopoly Capitalism, (London), Macmillan.

Garfinkel, H., (1963), A Conception of, and Experiments with "Trust" as a Condition of Stable Concerted Actions, in O.J. Harvey (ed), Motivation and Social Interaction; Cognitive Determinants, New York: Ronald Press.

Garfinkel, H., (1967), Studies in Ethnomethodology, Englewood Cliffs, New Jersey: Prentice-Hall.

Good, D., (1988), Individuals, Interpersonal Relations, and Trust, in D. Gambetta (ed), op cit, pp 31-48.

Groves, T., (1973), Incentives in Teams, Econometrica, Vol XLI, July, pp 617-631.

Hawthorn, G. , (1988), Three Ironies in Trust, in D. Gambetta (ed), op cit, pp 111-126.

Hirshleifer, J., (1956), On the Economics of Transfer Pricing, Journal of Business, July, pp 172-184.

Hirshman, A.O., (1984), Against Parsimony: Three Easy Ways of Complicating Some Categories of Economic Discourse, American Economic Review Proceedings, Vol 74, pp 88-96.

Hughes, C.L., (1965), Why Budgets Go Wrong, Personnel, Vol 42 (3), May-June, pp 16-26.

Jönsson, S., (1990), Accounting for Improvement, paper presented at the European Accounting Association, Budapest, April.

Jönsson, S. and Grönlund, A., (1988), Life with a Sub-Contractor: New Technology and Management Accounting, <u>Accounting, Organizations and Society</u>, Vol 13, (5), pp 512-532.

Knights, D. and Willmott, H.C., (1989), Power and Subjectivity at Work; From Degradation to Subjugation in Social Relations, <u>Sociology</u>, Vol 23 (4), pp 535-558.

Lorenz, E.H., (1988), Neither Friends nor Strangers: Informal Networks of Subcontracting in French Industry, in D. Gambetta (ed), op cit, pp 194-210.

Luhmann, N., (1979), Trust and Power, Chichester: Wiley.

Luhmann, N., (1988), Familiarity, Confidence, Trust: Problems and Alternatives", in D. Gambetta (ed), op cit, pp 94-107.

March, J.G. and Olsen, J.P., (1976), Organizational Learning and the Ambiguity of the Past, in J.G. March and J.P. Olsen (eds), Ambiguity and Choice in Organizations, Bergen: Universitetsforlaget, pp 54-68.

Meyer, J.W. and Scott, W.R., (1983), Organizational Environments, New York: Russell Sage.

Mintzberg, H., (1983), Power in and Around Organizations, Englewood Cliffs: Prentice Hall.

Morgan, G., (1986), Images of Organization, Beverley Hills: Sage.

Neu, D., (1991), New Stock Issues and the Institutional Production of Trust, <u>Accounting, Organizations and Society</u>, Vol 16 (2), pp 185-200.

Pollard, S., (1965), The Genesis of Modern Management, London: Edward Arnold.

Samuels, J.M., (1969), Penalties and Subsidies in Internal Pricing Policies, Journal of Business Finance.

Wildavsky, A., (1975), Budgeting: A Comparative Theory of Budgetary Processes, Boston: Little Brown.

Zand, D.E. (1972), Trust and Managerial Problem Solving, Administrative Science Quarterly, Vol 17 (2), pp 229-239.

Part 2

The Scientific Enterprise

THE ENGINE OF INQUIRY, or 'Why Say Anything at All?'

Richard J. Boland, Jr.
Case Western Reserve University

Abstract

This paper was begun during a year spent with Sten Jönsson at the Gothenburg School of Economics in 1988-89. The supportive, trusting atmosphere and the sense of openness to new ideas that Sten promotes in his department is in large part responsible for this essay or should I say 'to blame' for it. The thoughts reported here were induced by some qualities and interests of his that I was exposed to during that year. Among these I would particularly mention his respect for the actor/subject, his focus on the experience of the individual, his constant back and forth, in and out, up and down exploration of an issue, and his interests in cognitive structures, language and ghosts.

The paper asks why, once a question has been asked and an answer received, the conversation doesn't just stop? Why does it continue with another question and then another. The answer, I propose, is found in the reciprocal and metaphorical quality of language, especially as they operate in two orientational metaphors that frame and guide our conversations. The reciprocal structure of the multiple meanings of everyday language keep the conversation going, providing as it were, the Engine of Inquiry.

Introduction

The idea for this essay took shape during a morning hike with Knut Ims down a fiord northeast of Bergen. Our conversation that morning was about dialogue and the questions we asked were, 'what is good dialogue?' and 'how can good dialogue be designed?'. Early on in the conversation we discussed how, in the research each of us had been doing, the decision dialogue of experts differed from that of novices. While inquiring into a problem, novices seemed to skate along the surface of the problem space, moving quickly from one domain, or way of framing the problem, to another. Experts, in contrast, seemed to stay within a limited set of problem frames, but explored each frame in a richer, more complex way than the novice. Both the novice and the expert tended to raise new issues as they inquired into a problem space. But the expert seemed to raise new issues that elaborated on ideas within existing problem frames, whereas the novice seems to raise new issues by jumping to new framings of the problem.

For instance, in Boland, Greenberg, Park and Han (1990) a situation that could be framed as a marketing problem, a strategy problem, a finance problem, a personnel problem, or a problem of management will and motivation, was presented to both novice and expert decision makers. The experts would tend to develop sophisticated views within one or two framings of the situation. During decision dialogue they would add new elements or new relations to the analysis, thus generating new insights, but within the same framing of the problem. The novice, in contrast, would start with a problem statement that drew on a few initial framings, and in the process of decision dialogue would add new elements by shifting to new frames.

Given this general difference between the novice and the expert, our next question was whether one style of inquiry was in some sense superior to the other. Or, on the other hand, are each of them 'trapped' in a style of inquiry that was incomplete, and partial? Shouldn't good decision dialogue somehow be able to display both these patterns of exploring a problem space? Doesn't inquiry have to do with integrating both the child-like exploration of a problem by the novice, that can bring fresh perspectives to the situation, and the complex understanding of the expert that brings an intimate and subtle knowledge of particular parts of the problem space. The novice can help us break out of the familiar categories that tend to hold and localize our inquiry, while the expert can help us reject superficial understandings which might divert our inquiry from substantive issues.

Knut and I decided that good decision dialogue does require integrating these two voices, but probably does not mean integrating them in a strict alternating sequence. That would seem to be too mechanical. But, we thought, good decision dialogue should at least allow both to coexist as two voices in a conversation so that each could provide the answer to the problem of inquiry that seemed to be raised by the other. In the image of good decision dialogue that we developed during that morning walk, we thought that both voices should always be present - one sitting backstage to rescue the other from the traps of inquiry that befall the voice that is frontstage. The novice, as a childlike explorer of broad surfaces, rescues the expert when the expert has gone too far and can no longer see 'the forest for the trees'. The expert, in turn, brings the child-like novice back to earth, grounding its flights of fancy with precision, detail and complex attention to particulars.

There are many stories in the history of scientific inquiry showing this interplay of novice and expert voices (Beveridge, 1957; Koestler, 1964; Kuhn, 1962). The new entrant to a scientific field sees new relations that reframe old, seemingly irreconcilable details. Alternatively, the diligent expert, digging deeper into the implications of a theory, reveals anomalies that build up pressure to reconceive the basic problem statement being addressed. The question that remained for us was how can good decision dialogue, one that displayed this bi-vocal quality, be designed?

Engine of Inquiry

At this point in our discussion, Knut and I tried to reflect on our own dialogue as a process of inquiry. Our initial observation was how thoroughly metaphorical our thinking about decision dialogue had been. Metaphorical reference to space, surface, depth, forest and frame were everywhere in our talk. We were immersed in metaphors, to the point where they seemed to almost take over in shaping and guiding our thinking. It was at that moment in our discussion that the central idea of this paper emerged. Namely, we don't have to design a new kind of decision dialogue in order to have a structure that alternates between the narrowly focused, expert type of analysis and the broad ranging, novice type of exploration. The shared metaphors of the ordinary language we use to engage in inquiry and conduct our decision dialogue already has such a structure.

At any time in a decision dialogue, either the expert or the novice voice is in the frontstage and the very act of using it, pushing it further and working out its lines of inquiry, raises new problems. These new problems set the conditions for which the other voice is called upon as a solution. As the other voice moves frontstage, its very use again sets new kinds of problems and provides the conditions under which the other voice is turned to as the best hope for an answer. The metaphorical structure of our ordinary language keeps the conversation between these voices going in something like a perpetual motion machine. I will call this metaphorical structure the Engine of Inquiry.

In this paper I will discuss the metaphorical schemas that structure our decision dialogue and how they make movement between the two voices of the novice's surface exploration and the expert's depth analysis, inevitable. In order to do so, I will draw upon a concept of language and cognition put forward by Lakoff and Johnson (1981), and later developed by each separately (Lakoff, 1987; Johnson, 1987).

The Bodily Basis of Inquiring Dialogue

Lakoff and Johnson argue against an objectivist view of language and cognition and propose an experientialist alternative. The objectivist view holds that we can best find truth by clearly separating mind from body so that we might purify our language categories, strip away the bias of our subjectivity and reveal an objective core of meaning. Free from the bias of our subjectivity, this objective core of meaning would then enable us to use categories that truly reflect the world as it is and allow us to make reliably accurate representations of reality.

In place of this objectivist view and its program to guarantee knowledge by pursuing Descarte's dream of separating mind from body, Lackoff and Johnson propose a radical reframing of our basic notion of language and cognition. In the experientialist view they develop, our most elementary categories and schemas essentially depend upon and importantly emerge from our bodily experience. For them, our mind only has categories to work with in the first place because of our bodily experience. If mind were successfully separated from body in order to make it purely 'objective', it would be a mind devoid of categories and constructs. Johnson summarizes his argument against objectivism as follows:

"The key...is to focus on something that has been ignored and undervalued in objectivist accounts of meaning and rationality - the *human body*, and especially those structures of imagination and understanding that emerge from our embodied experience... The body has been ignored because it seems to have no role in reasoning about abstract subject matters".

"Yet, in all of the empirical studies cited above,...the embodiment of human meaning and understanding manifests itself over and over,...the kind of imaginative structuring uncovered in these studies...are forms of imagination that grow out of bodily experience, as it contributes to our understanding and guides our reasoning" (Johnson, 1987, pp XIV).

As Lakoff puts it:

- "Thought is embodied, that is, the structures used to put together our conceptual systems grow out of bodily experience and make sense in terms of it; moreover, the core of our conceptual systems is directly grounded in perception, body movement, and experience of a physical and social character".

- "Thought is imaginative in that those concepts which are not directly grounded in experience employ metaphor, metonymy, and mental imagery...The imaginative capacity is also embodied - indirectly - since the metaphors, metonomies, and images are based on experience, often bodily experience "(Lakoff, 1987, p XIV).

The Dynamic Interplay of Metaphors in Conversation

In their joint and separate works, Lakoff and Johnson present their analysis of imaginative structures (based on what they call 'image schemata') as a series of discrete metaphors or metaphorical complexes that occur in isolated phrases in our ordinary language. They do not explore the implications for the structuring of extended conversations, but instead focus on short, separate phrases to serve as examples of how image schematas emerge from bodily experience. What I propose to do in this paper is to put legs on their ideas, as it were, and to see where some important structuring metaphors go when we follow them through time in conversations. I want to consider how several of Lakoff and Johnson's embodied image schematas that structure the expert and the novice form of inquiry, interact dynamically over time as we engage in conversations.

The question that intrigues me here is why, so often, our decision dialogues keep going? Why, when a question is posed and an answer is given, doesn't the conversation just stop? There always seems to be another question that follows. After your question has been answered, why say anything at all?

What I hope to add to the themes explored by Lackoff and Johnson is a sense of how a few shared orientational metaphors that emerge at a preconceptual level from our experience of being embodied on this earth interact in dialogue to keep our inquiry going. The ability of metaphors to interact over time that concerns me here is made possible by the way that words are never univocal in their reference (Levine, 1985; Derrida, 1974). The metaphor that a particular word participates in or points us to is itself ambiguous and subject to change during a conversational episode. The type of change I am referring to here is a sudden shift from one metaphorical reference to another, as in a figure ground reversal. A word participating in one metaphorical complex will, through a process of dialogue, suddenly call another, quite different metaphorical relation of that word into play, and thereby change the framing schemata for the conversation.

Often, this kind of shift can be found in a humorous aside during a conversation. Henny Youngman, the classic American stand-up comedian is famous for a one line joke that exemplifies this shift. In the middle of a story, as if to use his wife as an example of the point he is making he says "take my wife...please!" For another example, we might find the term 'head' being used to frame a conversation as in 'he is the head of the class'. In this example the class is framed with the schema 'the body is a container' with 'head' as a part of the body metaphorically related to an individual in the class. Here, it might be used to identify an individual as the brains of the class. But 'head' is not univocal in its metaphorical reference. One could imagine, for instance, that during the conversion, the word 'head' was later linked to the 'journey' metaphor, and referred to the student being at the front of a group of travelers following a path. Here, being the 'head' of the class could refer to his role in leading a change effort - which may or may not be a positive reference. Or, one could imagine that later in conversation it was noted that the class was part of a sailing school that taught about motor boating and the correct nautical terms for the various parts of a boat. Here, reference to the 'head' of the class could be quite distasteful, or at the least would be more openly ambiguous.

The core bodily-based schemas I wish to explore in this paper have to do with (1) the 'body as a container' and its derivative 'idea as a container', especially the distinction of surface and deep in the container metaphor as it is used to frame our discussion of ideas and inquiry; and (2) the 'cycle of night and day' that we experience as alternating periods of light and dark, especially as we use the night and day cycle to frame our thinking about what we know and the quality of our knowledge.

Experience of the Body as a Container

Johnson (1987) argues persuasively that the experience of our bodies in earth-bound space and time provides us with a shared set of preconceptual, experiential schemas. A very basic example is the experience of our body as a container (Lakoff and Johnson, 1981, pp 29). Our skin is the boundary between the interior and the exterior of our body. Our metabolism concerns ingesting and excreting , inhaling and exhaling, protecting the warm inner core from fluctuations in outer temperatures, and generally keeping the contents and appearance of our bodily container in good order. We use the body as container schema, in turn, to generate a wide range of containment metaphors (Johnson, 1987, pp 30-40; Lakoff, 1987, pp 271-273) including many based on the 'idea as container' schema.

- That idea won't hold water.

- Your idea is full of holes.

- You have to tighten up your argument.

With the 'idea as container' schema we identify what is important, significant and enduring from what is superficial and temporary; what is true from what is false. We know 'deep in our heart' what is true, and we know 'not to judge a book by its cover'. We know that 'depth knowledge' is superior to 'surface knowledge'. Surface knowledge is superficial, whereas depth knowledge is sophisticated and thorough. When we really know something well, we have penetrated to the central truth of the matter.

- He's just touched the surface of that question.

- She's a deep thinker.

- Have we probed the issue deeply enough?

- You must get beneath the surface to understand the
   significance of this question.

These metaphors deriving from the 'idea as container' schema locate truth spatially, with the center of the container's space being the deepest, truest knowledge, and with the periphery or surface of the space being the less trustworthy kind of knowledge.

- The central point of his argument is...

- His thinking is really on the fringe of this issue.

- We need to get to the heart of the matter.

- Those ideas have been pushed to the sidelines.

Experience of Cycles of Night and Day

Johnson (1987, p 119-121) also identifies the bodily experience of earthly cycles such as day and night, the progression of seasons, the waxing and waning moon and so forth as a source of shared experiential schemas. We use these cycle schemas, especially the schema of night and day cycles to generate metaphors of knowledge and understanding. Day is sunny and light, night is dark. Day is clear, night is unclear. When we want to understand something better, we try to bring some light to the subject. When we really know something well, we are very bright. When we lack knowledge or are unsure, we are in the dark.

- I now understand it as clear as day.

- Maybe he can shed some light on the subject.

- I didn't know about it, because they kept me in the dark.

Daylight is safe. Things are familiar and unthreatening during the day. Night is dangerous, unfamiliar and frightening. Evil creatures hide during the day and prowl for victims at night. Good people rise early at first light and work untill dark, when their day is done.

- Let's wait to consider it in the light of day.

- His argument is murky and hard to follow.

A Metaphorical Conjunction

We can depict the 'container' and the 'night and day' schemas and their related metaphorical references as shown in Figure 1.

Schema	Lacking Knowledge	Having Knowledge
Container	Surface	Deep
Night and Day	Dark	Light

Figure 1. Two schemas of inquiry

The container schema uses a spatial metaphor. The larger the container the larger the space. Being in the center of the space means having a deep understanding or an in-depth knowledge. Being at the periphery of the space means merely having a surface understanding, or super-ficial knowledge. The night and day schema uses an illumination meta-phor. The larger the area of illumination, the larger the possible area of knowledge. Being in a more brightly illuminated area means having a better knowledge. Being in a darker area means having less knowledge.

In the container schema, when we are at the surface and lack knowledge, we want to go deeper to achieve knowledge. In the night and day schema, when we are in the dark and lack knowledge, we want to seek light to achieve knowledge (see Figure 2).

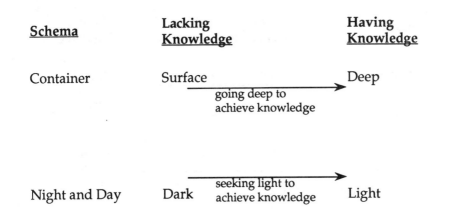

Schema	Lacking Knowledge		Having Knowledge
Container	Surface	going deep to achieve knowledge	Deep
Night and Day	Dark	seeking light to achieve knowledge	Light

Figure 2. Metaphorical referants for seeking knowledge

However, as discussed above, words such as light and deep have multiple referents. We have taken 'light' to serve as referent for the space metaphor of the 'container' schema and 'deep' to serve as referent for the illumination metaphor of the 'night and day' schema, but in our ordinary language usage of these words, they are not univocal.   These key words participate as referents in multiple metaphors. In this particular instance, I argue that the key words of each of these metaphorical structures participates in a subsidiary way in the other metaphor. That is, 'light' participates in <u>both</u> the illumination metaphor (as primary referent) <u>and</u> the spatial metaphor (as subsidiary referent). Similarly, 'deep' participates in <u>both</u> the spatial metaphor (as primary referent) <u>and</u> in the illumination metaphor (as subsidiary referent).

In order to seek knowledge, we try to cast light on a subject (primary referent), but light also refers to being light-weight, insubstantial, and superficial. Thus, it refers in a subsidiary way to the surface aspect of the container metaphor. Pushing too strongly toward the light or immersing oneself in the light increases the risk of going to far and becoming superficial and mere surface. This metaphorical reversal is shown in Figure 3.

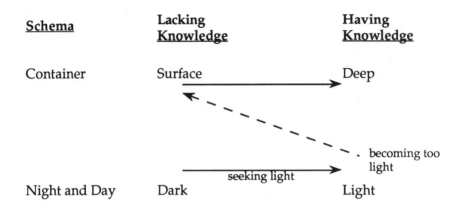

Figure 3. Switch of metaphorical referant from night and day to
         container schemas

Similarly, in order to seek knowledge we want to go deeper into a
subject (primary referent), but deep also refers to the most isolated and
darkest spot of a space and thus, in a subsidiary way to the dark aspect
of the illumination metaphor. Pushing too strongly toward a deep
understanding or overly embracing the deep increases the risk of going
too deep and becoming lost in the dark. Figure 4 depicts the reversal
from being deep in the container metaphor to being dark in the night
and day metaphor.

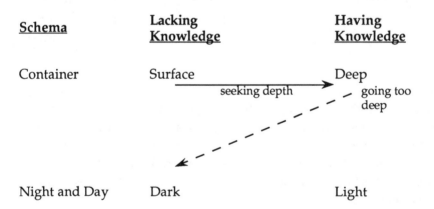

Figure 4. Switch of metaphorical referent from container to night and
         day schema

When we put these two sets of reciprocally related primary and subsidiary metaphorical referents together we have the Engine of Inquiry, a kind of perpetual motion machine for decision dialogue.

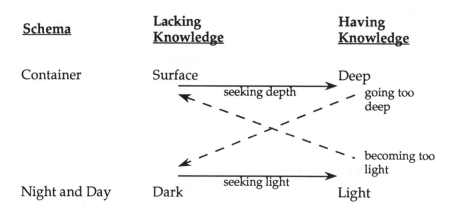

Figure 5. The Engine of Inquiry

In this system of reciprocally related metaphorical referents, the pursuit of inquiry through one metaphor brings with it a subsidiary reference that eventually increases in interpretive power and reframes the inquiry with an oppositely valent metaphor. Pursuing inquiry within one schema in order to increase knowledge creates the conditions that stimulate a switch to an alternative schema in which an awareness of our lack of knowledge is maximized, and the need for working toward knowledge in a new direction is most keenly felt.

A script for this interaction of schemas and their associated metaphorical framings over time is sketched below:

Schema	Framing of Inquiry
1. Container	We have merely superficial knowledge, we must go deep
2. Shift from Container to Night and Day	We have gone too deep, we are off the deep end and in the dark.
3. Night and Day	We are in the dark and must seek to shed light on it.
4. Shift from Night and Day to Container	We have become too light, all is superficial, we are merely at the surface.
5. Container	We have merely superficial knowledge; we must go deep
6. An so it goes...	

Implications

This paper has proposed a dynamic interrelationship between two schemas based on embodied experience that are commonly used to structure our inquiry during decision dialogue. The multivocal quality of words allows a term that serves as principal metaphorical referent under one schema to also serve as a subsidiary referent under another. In the dialogue of inquiry, the principal referents from each of the two commonly used schemas that have been identified ('idea as container' and 'cycle of night and day') also serve as subsidiary referents to the other. This reciprocal interdependency of principal and subsidiary referents, and their reversal during dialogue, creates a kind of perpetual motion machine I have called the Engine of Inquiry. Use of a metaphor associated with the 'idea as container' or 'cycle of night and day' schema creates conditions which tend to call the other metaphor and its associated schema into play, thereby reframing the inquiry.

Thus far, the Engine of Inquiry is just a proposal, though I hope it is an intuitively and experientially appealing one. The next step in the development of this idea would involve historical studies of selected domains of inquiry in management thought, trying to identify the experiential schemas and associated metaphors being drawn upon at various times during the continuing dialogue on particular issues. If the Engine of Inquiry proposal has merit, we should see key words shifting metaphorical referents and thereby calling alternative schemas into play over time. The schemas and related metaphors may be those discussed here, or they may be other experientially based ones. Such historical studies would therefore not just serve to confirm the relationships of the proposal, but could also serve to uncover other schemas and metaphors through which the Engine of Inquiry operates.

The value of the Engine of Inquiry proposal, if it proves to have interpretive power over a range of management inquiry, would be to question the nature of progress we make in our field of study, and hopefully to encourage a sense of humility in what we accomplish through decision dialogue.

Is it our ideas in themselves which we find so compelling, or their location in the metaphorical structuring of our conversations? When we assert that we have achieved a deep understanding of a topic, or have finally shed light on a subject, have we really made genuine progress? or have we just reached a turning point in the reframings of the Engine of Inquiry?

Acknowledgement

The author is grateful for many good dialogues with Knut Ims about this paper and thanks to Ted O'Leary for giving it a title.

References

Beveridge, I.B., (1957), The Art of Scientific Investigation, 3rd ed., New York: Norton.

Boland, R.J., Greenberg, R.H., Park, S.H., and Han, I., (1990), Mapping the Process of Problem Reformulation: Implication for Understanding Strategic Thought, Mapping Strategy Thought, Huff, A. (ed), Chichester: Wiley.

Derrida, J., (1974), White Mythology: Metaphor in the Text of Philosophy, New Literary History.

Johnson, M., (1987), The Body in the Mind: The Bodily Basis of Meaning, Imagination and Reason, Chicago: University of Chicago Press.

Koestler, A., (1964), The Act of Creation, New York: Macmillan.

Kuhn, T.S., (1962), The Structure of Scientific Revolution, Chicago: University of Chicago Press.

Lakoff, G., (1987), Women, Fire and Dangerous Things: What Categories Reveal About the Mind, Chicago: University of Chicago Press.

Lakoff, G. and Johnson, M., (1980), Metaphors We Live By, Chicago: University of Chicago Press.

Levine, D., (1985), The Flight from Ambiguity, Chicago: University of Chicago Press.

NICE WORK IN STRANGE WORLDS:
Anthropological Inspiration for Organization Theory

Barbara Czarniawska-Joerges
Lund University

When nobody can understand the whole organization,
when all actors just have fragments of images
of what the organization is or what it ought to be
- is it then reasonable to talk of one organization . . . ?
(Jönsson, 1982, p 6).

A Topic for Organization Studies

Out of 16 waking hours, at least eight are spent in organizations. The main source of power experienced by most people in ordinary situations resides there. The result is that even those remaining hours we think, fear, and reexperience the previous and the next organizational eight hours. Employing organizations are, for most people, the main source of identity. There are very few people in modern Western societies who do not share this fate: some who were not given the chance to join in, like the unemployed; some privileged dropouts, who can afford to stray outside, and some well-meaning alternative seekers who usually end up creating alternative organizations, often taking more than eight hours of people's daily life. To an increasing degree, organization becomes the most indicative aspect of the modern, Western, way of life.

What understanding of this phenomenon do we have? Our knowledge of organizations is somewhat obsolete. Firstly, we have the 19th century ideal types, like in analyses of Weber or Marx, which continue to serve as a source of intellectual inspiration, but become more and more distant from the reality which we observe around us (or on our

TV-screens). Their interpretative power diminishes. Secondly, we have various normative models, applying to different kinds of activities within organizations: political science models for political and public sector organizations, economic models for business organizations. Their relevance for understanding organizations is weak: the main assumption made is that organizations are purposefully created to realize the goals typical for a given kind of activity. This narrowly rationalist perspective bursts at the seams when used for interpretative aims. Finally, then, we have various kinds of descriptive, empirical studies which try to represent processes which can be put together under the name of "organizing" (on advantages of using the term "organizing" rather than "organization", see Weick, 1979). In relation to the totality of social life, "organizing" is a matter of degree: at one extreme would be sets of processes recognized under a common name of "formal organizations", on the other, solitary activities with no obvious connections to collective action (say, dying or watching the sea). Here we are speaking then of interpretative studies of processes close to the first extreme.

This last type of study seems, naturally, to offer most possibilities for understanding the phenomenon that might be seen as central in modern culture (Czarniawska-Joerges, 1991). (From here on, I use the term "culture" in an old-fashioned way - to denote all that is created by humankind. It does not follow, though, that its opposite is nature. This uneasy dualism, typical for modern thinking, has produced more problems than solutions. For the purposes of this paper let us assume that culture is a bubble created by us within which we live - and although we recognize much of what we see as not made by us, we see it always as covered with the filmy surface of our bubble).

Organizations are thus the way the bubble is predominantly formed. However, our understanding of this formation is, on the one hand, unsystematic (the organization-as-a-way-of-life studies are still not that many); on the other hand, it comes to a great extent from times before the true onset of large, complex organizations and large technical systems. The ethnographic accounts come most often from small organizations or from manageable units of large organizations (there are some obvious reasons for it and some less obvious ways of dealing with the problem to which I shall return later). We need to understand large organizations as our way of life and we need a way to foster this understanding.

Here are the two first reasons for turning to anthropology for inspiration. In the first place, organization theory can be quite legitimately seen as a part of anthropology if anthropology is a discipline that is devoted to studying culture (I am not unaware that with this kind of definition most disciplines would be part of anthropology). In the second place, anthropology as a way of knowing has to offer experiences that are more interesting that those of other disciplines. In sections to follow I shall examine several of these advantages.

A Three-Dimensional Organization

Sometimes the negative examples are most telling. Let me then begin by describing problems that organization theory encounters while looking for inspiration in four disciplines which are traditionally seen as most appropriate models for this eclectic field: economics, psychology, political sciences and sociology. (In doing that, I will be using the mainstream models: within each of these disciplines there is a vibrant margin that is actually leaning in a similar direction to the present paper, and I will mention these as well).

Economics is the most legitimate source of theory and method for organization theory. Organizations, however, are treated as an abomination in a pure science of economics. A truly economic behavior, that is, utility-maximizing choices, enters in an aggregated form the institution of the market to be processed there. Legitimate organizing happens, basically, in two places only: in production and in banks. These, in their turn, should act basically as a collective rational decision-maker, i e maximize their own utility function. "Organizations as a way of life" is an odd way of phrasing the problem in this tradition. Either the "way of life" is all that happens outside economic behavior, or else it should be subordinated to the same laws, whereby the problem is redundant.

From my presentation of economics it should clearly appear that psychology approaches the same phenomena in a very similar way, only at a micro-level. The cognitive-oriented, rationalistic and behaviorist psychology for many decades went hand in glove with economics, explaining the determinants of economic behavior and the deviations from it.

The political sciences helped organization theory to make a move toward reality by introducing the concept of different interests which become politically united or opposed (lobbying and negotiations replace, to some extent, the aggregative gain-maximization where differences are solved automatically by the market mechanism). This perspective, however, was painlessly incorporated into economic models by either assuming that organizations select people with the same interest (or at least willing to adopt the same interest) or else, that conflict of interests can be solved by negotiation and consensus reaching, whereupon the collective actor proceeds to maximize its gains.

Finally, the most problematic of all, sociology. Part of the problem lies, of course, in an uneasy relation between anthropology and sociology (which is a subdiscipline of which?), but this part I can omit limiting myself to relationships between sociology and organization theory. These are, as it were, of markedly local and temporary character. In many academic communities (for example Sweden and Germany) sociology was seen as an inevitably critical discipline, and therefore highly unsuitable as a model for, basically apologetic, organization theory. In other contexts (for example Great Britain and the U S A) sociologists were those who created organization theory and ran it, so to speak: organization theory is seen as a part of sociology. In the latter case, organization theory repeated the main dilemma of its mother-discipline: the duality of the individual and the system, the impossibility of treating the social on its proper terms.

With such models to follow, no wonder that contemporary organization theory, lavish with approaches and overflowing with tolerance, still has basic problems with grasping the idea of "social". Whenever organizations are not mechanisms, organisms or something of the sort, they are usually aggregates of persons (like in organizational psychology) or else Supra-Persons who "decide", "learn", "interpret" (see, for an interesting example, Daft and Weick, 1984). Although we know that organizations are not really persons, for all practical purposes they are treated as such.

And yet their social character is, in my opinion, the key to their understanding. Here anthropology is most helpful as, maybe due to its overconcern with small societies and at the same time lack of close contact with individuals populating them, it was forced to focus on the social character of life.

How can one grasp the social character of life? Rom Harré proposes that

. . . the public and collective aspects of human life are to be treated as product generated by an interplay between a practical order, concerned with the production of the means of life, and an expressive order concerned with honour and reputation (Harré, 1979, p 4, emphasis added).

Although I find this definition of expressive order peculiarly masculine (I would speak about "dignity and meaningfulness"), I would agree with this interpretation of becoming of the social order, and also with the addition that "for most people at most times the expressive order dominates or shapes the practical order" (p 4).

Abner Cohen (1974), answering Marcuse's challenge of one-dimensionality of modern human life, proposed a two-dimensional picture: a political aspect combined with a symbolic one. Going further, one might look at this particular set of social processes which is called "complex organization", as a composition of practical, symbolic and political dimensions.

While attending to their practical and expressive needs, people produce relationships between themselves which persist over many a social and organizational action. Think, if you will, of the political axis as a relatively static one, with the other two creating it through their related dynamics. The direction one chooses depends on personal beliefs, especially those concerning politics, on understanding organizations. But the three must remain together if the whole of organizational life is to be portrayed.

This way of reasoning about organizations necessarily puts the analysis in between the macro and micro levels, between "individuals" and "social structures", on a meso, or middle-range level. Leaving the micro-level is necessary if we assume that a collective (or a group) reveals characteristics not inherent in any of its parts, and this indeed is an assumption on which organizations were built. But what about social classes, economic systems and historical forces?

Harré's analysis (1981) deals with people on all levels, from individuals to societies. The difference between micro, meso and macro was originally the difference in numbers. His reasoning can be, however, extended to the case where organizations are seen as sets of processes and not as groups of persons.

Harré's argument was, in short, that macro-groupings had no structural properties (relations between elements which were not properties of elements themselves) and therefore could be, at best, seen as taxonomic groupings (every member shares the same property, for example, blue eyes or a Swedish passport) and treated as rhetorical devices. (Abner Cohen said, in the same vein, that "classes are figments of the imagination of sociologists", 1974, p 17).

Harré claimed that the only way to study collectives was by applying an ethogenic methodology which "involves assembling members' understandings and interpretations of the institution and the events which make up its life, and negotiating these with an outside observer's ethnography" (1981, p 151).

If we agree with the above postulate, which I do, then it becomes clear that it is not only the anthropological method that is to be used, but also an anthropological theory, or frame of reference. The anthropological theory which, in my opinion, forms the most fruitful frame of reference for organization studies is the one that sees reality as socially constructed.

Social Construction of Organizational Reality

It is often assumed that collective action, and thus, obviously, organizational action, requires shared meaning. This is correct to a certain extent (to carry a table together we must be of the same opinion on what is up and what is down; what is forward and what is back). However, a collective action is possible in the face of many meanings which are only partly shared. It is the experience of a given collective action which is shared, more than its meaning. Two municipal officials attended the same conference organized by the Swedish Association of Local Governments. In describing this event to me, one portrayed the main speaker as "a visionary who gives you a will to shape the future according to your dreams" whereas the other commented that "it was a rehash of old platitudes". They are, nevertheless, members of the same complex organization (or, more correctly, a constellation of organizations) and what was common for them was that they went to the same place at the same time, sharing an expectation that the experience might be useful and relevant for them. (For a similar view on shared meanings, see Weick, 1979 and Donnellon et al, 1986).

Organizations (and not only their environments, as Smircich and Stubbart, 1985, claim) are therefore daily enacted and socially constructed, due to the fact that any collective action requires a shared element of meaning. Meanings are thus created (both in social interactions and in interactions with artifacts and nature), deconstructed, negotiated, elaborated.

Reality as we daily experience it is socially constructed. Every building is socially constructed: it consists of bricks, mortar, human labor, building law, architectural design, aesthetic expression and so on, each of them in turn socially constructed and put together by a socially constructed concept of a building.

Which means that reality exists, independently of human perception, but it is not "out there", behind a wall of "human distortion" that must be overcome, but "in here", where the human perception is a part of it, a maker of it, and the only tool for its cognition. These limits of our cognition may be lamentable, but only from some transcendental point of view; otherwise, as human perception is the basis for human praxis, it is sufficient in terms of this praxis, and it still evolves, technologically and maybe psychologically, helping praxis to evolve.

Which means that the rain would still fall down on the earth if there were no humans to watch it, only that this fact would be then irrelevant to the human race, as it could not be socially (re)constructed. And the reverse: that shutting one's eyes, living entirely on illusions and wishful thinking does not stop people being killed daily as the villains and the heroes continue their contribution to social construction. Reality is therefore "a quality appertaining to phenomena that we recognize as having a being, independent of our own volition (we cannot 'wish them away')" (Berger and Luckmann, 1966/1971, p 13).

Organizations are socially constructed - and reconstructed - in everyday actions. Organizations can also be destroyed by action, but it will again be a case of social destruction. It does not mean that organizations exist only in our imagination. We cannot "wish them away". But if nobody came to work anymore, a factory would become "that old factory building".

How to study social constructions? By "sorting out the structures of signification (...) and determining their social ground and import" (Geertz, 1973, p 9). A translation into hermeneutical terms (which I tend to use) would result in saying that we shall explicate the constructions we find and explore the ways they were constructed. The ways of writing it up are then many and varied, as Geertz shows in his book on the anthropologist as author (1988), but at present we can put this problem aside. The issue of social construction hastened the discussion from that which is to be analyzed to the analysis itself. Before that can take place, though, there is another moment of significance - the field.

The Uses of Exoticism

A common enemy of field research within a native society is the "taken-for-grantedness" of meanings and their modes of construction. In fact, it has been invariably postulated within anthropology that this hindrance makes studies of "own culture" ("a culture" being a local and temporal variation of culture) meaningless. Leach (1985), for example, is, "at the cost of being accused of being old-fashioned" against anthropologists studying their own cultures:

. . . fieldwork in a cultural context of which you already have intimate first-hand experience seems to be much more difficult than fieldwork which is approached from the naive viewpoint of a total stranger. When anthropologists study facets of their own society their vision seems to become distorted by prejudices which derive from private rather than public experience (1982, p 124).

It is hard not to agree with this observation. On the other hand, for most researchers complex organizations (other than their own) are almost as exotic as the Trobrianders' community. Peggy Reeves Sanday sends her students to restaurants or fire stations, and says: "My experience with these students has been that it is possible to train those who are highly motivated to see the world from another's point of view without sending them to exotic foreign lands" (1979, p 528). Desensitivization or bias comes more distinctly into the picture when the context has to be taken into account, the society as a whole. But this has to be contrasted with an outsider's clumsy ignorance which is removed only after a complete acculturation. If such is at all possible:

Much nonsense has been written, by people who should know better, about the anthropologist "being accepted". It is sometimes suggested that an alien people will somehow come to view the visitor of distinct race and culture as in every way similar to the locals. This is, alas, unlikely. The best one can probably hope for is to be viewed as a harmless idiot who brings certain advantages to this village (Barley, 1983/1986, p 56).

When it is not a village but a corporation, the natives sometimes share this illusion of a common culture for a brief moment ("You, coming from the School of Economics, would surely see that..."). But even Nigel Barley's Dowayos thought that he was a reincarnated spirit of a sorcerer who put off his white skin whenever he want to sleep These tender illusions do not remove the basic sense of alienation which is obvious in a prolonged contact. With luck, one can be seen as "an uninformed but well-willing researcher", a euphemism for a "harmless idiot".

Additionally, studies of organizations in other countries can be extremely useful in the sense that they challenge the "taken-for-grantedness" of one's own culture. Ethnomethodology proposed breaking down the tight social tissue by a purposeful act of rebellion as a remedy for taken-for-grantedness. This has, obviously, many advantages in special situations. However, it also produces anger and frustration (like in Garfinkel's famous experiments, 1967). Moreover, in order to challenge the taken-for-grantedness in an ethnomethodo–logical way, the researcher must have already done it beforehand. I cannot problematize that what is unproblematic to me.

An anthropological study of an organization, in its prolonged contact with the field, reveals immediately what many a young researcher tries to hide: that organizations are strange worlds for those who live in academia. This revelation might never take place when sporadic contacts form the basis of empirical knowledge: equipped with preconceptions, the students of organization "collect" that which fits their models, very much as illustrated in the saying that "to one who has the hammer, the world is made of nails".

A field study is, in many ways, an experience similar to that of immigration. First of all, the similarity lies in the fact that field workers, like immigrants, have to be re-socialized. They have to undergo a process which is much more painful than that of the original socialization, because it inevitably means a clash between different socialization rules, or simply speaking, between two cultures. From that follows a second similarity: the identity of a person, taken for granted by successfully functioning adults, becomes challenged. A student of organization, like an immigrant, perceives that new people she meets try to reconstruct her image, to classify her personality, which requires conscious monitoring of self-presentation and a generally increased self-reflection, operations which, one hoped, were safely put away together with other memories of adolescence. Thirdly, the feeling of "being dumb", of continually running into glass walls, if less acute in a study compared to immigration experience, is also basically the same.

Many researchers who consider themselves empirical students of organizations may not recognize this picture at all. In numerous cases that can be due to a successful employment of defence mechanisms protecting the exposed egos. Like immigrants who retire to their families looking for relics of the old culture, so do they, only more easily so, retreat to their own culture and forget about the discomfort caused by the encounter with aliens. Non-anthropological, "aerial" methods of data gathering facilitate this evasion. A telephone interview shields one from the embarassed face of the respondent as the interviewer makes a terrific blunder, and strange noises can be blamed on line failure. But even the necessity of meeting a respondent twice provides researchers with personal feedbacks which they might wish to avoid. All that feels most acute when one has to reside in an organization and, so to speak, to earn one's daily social bread from day to day, which happens to some degree in any type of direct and repetitive contact. Some researchers are lucky enough to cut off the feeling of estrangement completely; the question arises whether their studies profit to the same degree. The psychological discomfort of estrangement that must be overcome seems to me a necessary price of learning. The bonus is in gaining extra knowledge about oneself; the main result - a problematized picture of organizational reality, which carries a promise of liberation for those who suffer under the constructed reality, and a non-trivial story for the researcher.

Adaptations and Compromises

How much of a large organization can one person understand after a year of sitting in one position? Very much, as Dalton's (1959) example shows. However, both Dalton's situation in the company and his skill in method can be seen as due to luck rather than to careful design. The understanding of a large organization from any one position inside is limited by definition - large organizations are those which are not any longer understood by their own actors, as the initial quote from Sten Jönsson (1982) indicates. On the other hand, the probability of meeting a sponsor who will wish to finance several persons for several years of full-time study can be counted together with miracles. Pragmatic solutions must be looked for.

One of them is what I called an "observant participation", a method I proposed and introduced in a study of a consumer goods management system in Poland (Beksiak and Czarniawska, 1977; Czarniawska 1980). The study consisted of several stages, but in each of them actors in chosen organizations (from 10 to 25 at a time) were, under our guidance, collecting systematic observations of events over a period of 1,5 years. We would never have achieved an insertion of 25 researchers in organizations of the same branch, and if so, we might have waited 1,5 years for them to be acculturated enough to be able to start observation.

I still use this method with variations, as it has proven fruitful, often in a variation that can be called, after Stephen Barley (1983) "ethnographic interviews": repetitive (over a period of one year or longer), open and extensive interviews aiming at achieving a representation of people's work and organization.

But there is a very serious mistrust of interviews within the anthropological method. By interviewing people we learn about the reality of interviewing, and not about some other reality behind, say the ethnomethodologists. By interviewing people we create an artificial reality which does not relate to the "real" reality, say the ethnographers. By interviewing people about something we miss an authentic insight, say the phenomenologists.

All this is true, but also exaggerated. Giving answers to the interviewers, as long as it reveals a pattern, is a part of making sense in (and of) organizations. In other words, if organizational actors lie, and they do it in a repetitive way, this common lie is more informative than an idiosyncratic truth. There may be no other reality behind the interview, but the respondents believe there is, and we want to reconstruct their beliefs. And, finally, enriching as the observation might be, it will never be comprehensive without the actor's accounts, and what are interviews if not provoked accounts?

According to Scott and Lyman (1968), an account is

. . . a linguistic device employed whenever an action is subjected to valuative inquiry . . . a statement made by a social actor to explain unanticipated or untoward behavior - whether that behavior is his own or that of others, and whether the proximate cause for the statement arises from the actor himself or from someone else (p 46).

I am not sure whether Scott and Lyman would agree, but in my view, almost all behavior is unanticipated for someone in an anthropological frame of mind, and therefore an account of organizational action can be legitimately demanded. Usually, the actors understand this estrange–ment and willingly produce desired accounts (although they do say sometimes "Don't they teach you all that at your business school?", refusing to acknowledge the researcher's lack of social competence).

My claim that interviews are provoked accounts is based on the fact that organizational action, from the point of view of lay persons, or from the perspective of rules of everyday life, appears peculiar, and therefore has to be accounted for, usually in terms of rationality (whereas the everyday accounts are more often formulated in terms of morality). Additionally, this need to account for one's actions might not be so natural in the face of participant observers who, by virtue of participation, are supposed to share, at least to some degree, the same values and norms. Actually, the old anthropologists were not really participating; they were observers, and as such permitted to demand accounts and to obtain them. One can repeat after Hannah Arendt, who was speaking out of her personal and social experience, that:

In matters of theory and understanding, it is not uncommon for outsiders and spectators to gain a sharper and deeper insight into the actual meaning of what happens to go on before or around them than it would be possible for the actual actors or participants, entirely absorbed as they must be in the events (Young-Bruehl, 1982, p xi)

The point is trivial: all techniques have advantages and disadvantages. As the interview can be seen as the most accessible technique for research in organizations, our interest lies in maximizing the former and minimizing the latter.

Anthropology as a Frame of Mind

The anthropological method, then, is not so much a question of techniques (one might well perform the operation of participative observation completely insulated) as a certain readiness of mind and heart, as it were. I would claim that one can study the most exotic cultures and find nothing more than the image that emerged from above the desk at home; one can study an organization next door and find wonders of unparalleled exoticism. What is it that constitutes the difference?

As it is very often the case, the metaphoric examples can convey the meaning with much more strength than lengthy discussions. I am therefore going to make my point by using an illustration excerpted from a novel by David Lodge, called "Nice Work". The story told in the novel is an epitome of anthropological work with its promises and traps alike.

Robyn, a postfeminist, poststructuralist academic, lives truly in a two-dimensional world, that is, the world of symbols and politics (the latter both in a positive sense of the feminist movement, and the negative one, the politics of academia). Prompted by the latter, she enters another world - that of the industry. Her partner in that world, the Managing Director Vic, lives similarly in a two-dimensional world, the two dimensions being the political and the practical one. Symbols do not exist for Vic; practical things do not exist for Robyn.

Robyn is determined to make her visit a non-anthropological one. She plans to colonize the other world, taking for granted that her world contains all the concepts and tools needed to dismantle the other. For Vic, her visit is an intrusion that has to be tolerated (for company-political reasons) but he has no fear of colonization. Vic takes his world to be the only correct one: he takes it for granted. Thus Robyn's feeling of superiority: as a poststructuralist, she knows better than that. Or so she thinks - Lodge is showing us that, although she relativizes Victor's world, she takes her own world for granted just like Victor.

Lodge opens his book with a quote from Disraeli ("Sybil or the Two Nations"):

Two nations; between whom there is no intercourse and no sympathy; who are as ignorant of each other's habits, thoughts and feelings, as if they were dwellers in different zones, or inhabitants of different planets; who are formed by a different breeding, and fed by different food, and ordered by different manners . . .

This is, however, the author's and the reader's perspective. The two characters do not see themselves as belonging to different worlds: they are inhabitants of the same country in the same time; it is their professions that differ, but surely people from different professions live together in close symbiosis? The encounter proves to be a shock to both of them, the realization - at first accompanied by negative feelings - of the completedness and estrangement of the other world, then curiosity and finally mutual learning and respect.

The result of their encounter is that each of them remains in their appropriate world, but this world is enriched, with a new dimension added, which, although it adapts uneasily to the rest, cannot be conveniently forgotten or removed. Victor enters the world of symbols and is never again going to see the ad for "Silk Cut" cigarettes with naive eyes. Robyn will live with the memory of the hell - the foundry - that she visited, which shall replace her image of industry straight from the Victorian novels. What is more, Vic's insistence on exchanging the roles - he becoming an anthropologist and visiting university - completes experience by reinterpreting even Robyn's world (an experience not unknown in the annals of anthropology - that of natives visiting "their" researchers at their home-base and unravelling the social webs at amazing speed).

Lodge's characters are forced, by a turn of events, to become anthropologists, and the gains they earn from this somewhat unsettling experience are precisely those which one hopes will crown the efforts of anthropologists in general:

It is to enlarge the possibility of intelligible discourse between people quite different from one another in interest, outlook, wealth, and power, and yet contained in a world where, tumbled as they are into endless connection, it is increasingly difficult to get out of each other's way (Geertz, 1988, p 147).

There is, of course, a risk of unfruitful encounters - like if anthropologists should wish to insist on the myth of the salvational powers of "science" (Geertz, 1988); if organization theorists should try to mechanically apply anthropology's "bag of tricks" - technical solutions without understanding for perspective. Now, however, when social sciences in general are freeing themselves from the (self-imposed) slavery of natural sciences, the time for encounters has come.

References

Barley, N., (1983), The innocent anthropologist, Harmondsworth, Mddx.: Penguin.

Barley, S. R., (1983), Semiotics and the study of occupational and organizational cultures, Administrative Science Quarterly, 28: pp 393-413.

Beksiak, J. and Czarniawska, B., (1977), Enterprise response patterns under the socialist management system, Oeconomica Polona, 2: pp 211-228.

Berger, P. and Luckmann, T., (1971), The social construction of reality, Harmondsworth, Mddx.: Penguin, [1966].

Bruner, J., (1986), Actual minds, possible worlds, Cambridge, MA: Harvard University Press.

Cohen, A., (1974), Two-dimensional man: An essay on the anthropology of power and symbolism in complex society, Berkeley: University of California Press.

Czarniawska, B., (1980), Metody badan i usprawnien procesu zarzadzania organizacjami gospodarczymi. IOZDiK, Materialy i Studia, 15.

Czarniawska-Joerges, B., (1992), Exploring Complex Organizations: A Cultural Perspective, Newbury Park, C A: Sage.

Daft, R.L. and Weick, K.E., (1984), Toward a model of organizations as interpretation systems, Academy of Management Review, 9(2): pp 284-295.

Dalton, M., (1959), Men who manage, New York: Wiley.

Donnellon, A., Gray, B. and Bougon, M.G., (1986), Communication, meaning and organized action, Administrative Science Quarterly, 31(1): pp 43-55.

Edelman, M., (1988), Constructing the political spectacle, Chicago: University of Chicago Press.

Garfinkel, H., (1967), Studies in ethnomethodology. Englewood Cliffs, N.J.: Prentice-Hall.

Geertz, C., (1973,) The interpretation of cultures, New York: Basic Books.

Geertz, C., (1988), Works and lives: The anthropologist as author, Stanford, CA: Stanford University Press.

Harré, R., (1979), Social being, Oxford: Basil Blackwell.

Harré, R., (1981), Philosophical aspects of the macro-micro problem. In: Knorr-Cetina, K. and Cicourel, A.V. (Eds.) Advances in social theory and methodology, Boston: Routledge and Kegan Paul.

Janowitz, M., (1963), Anthropology and the social sciences. <u>Current Anthropology</u>, 4(2): 139, pp 149-154.

Jönsson, S., Beksiak, J. & Czarniawska, B., (1978), Beteendemönster hos företag i en socialistisk ekonomi - Polen 1972-1975, <u>Erhvervs-økonomisk Tidsskrift</u>, 1.

Jönsson, S., (1982), A city administration facing stagnation. Political organization and action in Gothenburg, Stockholm: Swedish Council for Building Research.

Latour, B., (1989), One more turn after the social turn... Dialectics revisited, Paper prepared for the symposium at Reilly, October.

Leach, E.R., (1982), Social anthropology. Oxford: Oxford University Press.

Leach, E.R., (1985), Observers who are part of the system. The Times Higher Education Supplement, 29 November.

Lodge, D., (1988), Nice work, London: Penguin.

McCloskey, D.N., (1986), The rhetoric of economics, Brighton, Sussex: Harvester [1985].

McCloskey, D.N., (1987), Storytelling in economics, Stencil, August.

Perrow, Ch., (1989), A society of organizations, Stencil, July.

Sanday, PR., (1979), The ethnographic paradigm(s), <u>Administrative Science Quarterly</u>, 1979, 24(4), pp 527-538.

Scott, M.B. and Lyman, S.M., (1968), Accounts, <u>American Sociological Review</u>, 33, pp 46-62.

Smircich, L. and Stubbart, Ch., (1985), Strategic management in an enacted world, <u>Academy of Management Review</u>,10(4), pp 724-736.

Weick, K.E., (1979), The social psychology of organizing, Reading, MA: Addison-Wesley, [1969].

Weick, K.E., (1985), Sources of order in underorganized systems: Themes in recent organization theory, In: Lincoln, Y.S. (Ed.) Organizational theory and inquiry, Beverly Hills, CA: Sage.

Young, Bruehl, E., Arendt H., (1982), For the love of the world, New Haven: Yale University Press.

INTERACTIVE RESEARCH ON ORGANIZATIONS
- Applying a Temporary System Metaphor

Rolf A. Lundin
Umeå School of Business

Abstract

Based on the notion that research may be conceived of as an interactive endeavour, where the relevant interaction occurs between the researcher and people ordinarily working for the organization under study, we arrive at the temporary system metaphor for doing research. Applying principles of managing by projects in doing research and fulfilling all the goals of a research project may be useful, but is nevertheless in various ways problematic.

In this essay we allude to the temporary system metaphor of doing research and argue that by using this metaphor, we can introduce a new level of researcher deliberateness and consciousness.

Interactive Research and the Metaphor

Research on systems of human beings, like businesses, can be described as an interactive endeavour. This is certainly true by definition if some form of action research is planned and the researcher is working according to the Lewin prescription studying the object as a disturbed system (Lewin, 1954). In action research, the researcher acts with the explicit intention to change the real system in focus. The assumption is, of course, that the system will respond to these efforts. Furthermore, it is assumed that responses will help the researcher to discover or uncover fundamental mechanisms. Thus perceived, action research involves intervention experiments, with the dual purpose of effecting change and at the same time testing hypotheses (Argyris & Schön, 1991). The intention to change implies that the researcher not only takes responsibility for the research but also that she accepts and takes over responsibilities for the organization as such under study.

Even if the researcher has no intention whatsoever to disturb the organization, far less of taking over any responsibility for it, she is still likely by her mere presence to cause reactions among its members, invoke behavioral changes and excert an influence over the stream of significant events. At the same time the sequential character of the research effort will make her adapt her behavior over time. In other words, doing research might be thought of as a social act or a sequence of social episodes. Thus, "interactive research" might be an appropriate label for many research efforts where businesses or other organizations are involved (Lundin & Wirdenius, 1990).

If one accepts the general notion of interactive research, there should be several behavioral as well as conceptual implications for the researcher and the researched. One way to consider the relations between the researcher and the researched is in terms of a temporary system. Research viewed in this way implies that during the initial phases of a study, we are adding a temporary "research appendix" to the organization under study. From that point the appendix and the organization being scrutinized in various ways form one unit. Whatever the researcher and the researched do has implications for the new unit as a whole. Access and exit are the formal brackets delimiting the temporary appendix. Here we purport to illustrate how the researcher can conceive of his effort by applying the temporary system metaphor.

As to the expression, the word "temporary" of course has to do with the delimitation in time. All research projects are assumed to have a distinct start when the research effort is initiated and an equally distinct end when the efforts are ended (or when research funds have been spent). "System" similarly has to do with the delimitation in space. Even though some researchers appear to have an intention to change the world, most of us only succeed to change if anything only a minor part thereof.

However, neither delimitation in time nor in space is guaranteed even though intended, which leaves us with the notion of the "metaphor".

The temporary system metaphor is very much akin to the "ethnographic experience" (cf Reeves Sanday, 1983). Ethnographic work on site implies arranging a temporary system with very distinct entry and exit phases. However, we prefer the expression "temporary system metaphor" not only to the ethnographic terms (ethnographers do not include analysis and synthesis) but also to "researcher's role management" (Marshall & Rossman, 1989, pp 63 - 75) since role management appears one-sided according to the descriptive expression. Using the metaphor certainly involves a simplification of the interactive problem or possibility. However, by applying that simple metaphor from the very beginning (or at the initiation) of a research effort and subsequently, we might be able to handle interactions in a more conscious way. To illustrate this reasoning, experiences from a recent case study will be discussed.

Experiences from a Case Study

The basis for the illustration is a longitudinal case study performed by a collegue and myself and reported elsewhere (Lundin & Wirdenius, 1989) about renewal in a family-owned business in the construction industry. Before getting into details of specific interest in the present context, there is a need to spell out some fundamental features of the study.

It is longitudinal in the sense that it was initiated in 1985 and brought to a halt in 1989 when our book was published. In the meantime we were spending a considerable amount of time not only interviewing key actors in the company, participating in company meetings and collecting other material of relevance for the case, but also analyzing and synthesizing observations.

We had been puzzled by the obvious and well known conservative posture in the construction industry, so when the opportunity came along to study in some detail renewal efforts of the newly appointed CEO of this particular family business, the Diös group, with some 4 000 employees, we gladly accepted that challenge. The new CEO, who had the very difficult task to turn the problem-ridden family business around, had been externally recruited and was virtually unknown to the people in the company. However, he had participated in a previous study, so my collegue knew him fairly well.

Even though the new CEO was backed up by the main owner and company founder, the more than 90 years old mr Diös himself, the newly appointed CEO soon encountered difficulties in his efforts to renew the business. Like the rest of the construction industry, the business had experienced hardships during the last few years, and the company was in the red. Furthermore, the company culture was in various ways perpendicular to his style of management. In various ways his personality did not fit well with the family business situation. Some of the measures he took to turn the company around were regarded with suspicion. In fact, he even was met with open resistance from some of the managers of the subsidiaries when he tried to adapt the organization to fit his ideas of how to run the company.

Among the measures the CEO took to renew the company was to open up the fairly closed family business system through the use of external consultants. He further initiated a problem detection study and had consultants scrutinize the organizational setting in general and the system for economic control in particular. With the assistance of the de-facto owner, the elderly entrepreneur, mr Diös, he set up a new board of directors consisting mainly of experts or executives from the outside. In that way most members of the family and "friends" of the family were excluded.

The elderly, but very dominant company founder, mr Diös, "unexpectedly" died during the summer of 1986 at the age of 95. (The word "unexpectedly" is justified since everybody had come to think of mr Diös as immortal. He had been around since the company started operations in 1921 and at the age of 95 he was still very active in the company. He regularly visited construction sites and rumours said he was still coming to his office seven days a week.) During the summer of 1986 the turnaround efforts of the new CEO seemed to be paying off. With the help of generally improving business conditions in Sweden the company was back into making a profit. However, through owner action the CEO and "half the company board" were ousted during the autumn of 1986. (Since this happened in October we have named the incident the October revolution.) The owner group, now consisting of a dozen of the grandchildren of mr Diös activated the ownership function and took charge, appointed their own CEO, a previous member of the board and changed the company policies to fit the general notion of going public and getting the company's shares listed on the stock exchange.

Our work had been concentrating on the renewal efforts of the ousted CEO and the responses to his measures. The revolution implied that company interests in that kind of renewal activities dissipated. Renewal efforts were instead concentrated to the needs of the ownership group and directed towards making it possible for those of them who wished to do so to liquidate their holdings. Having established good contacts with key actors in the company including the most recent CEO we were fortunate to be able to complete our study in this phase of development with the new regime.

Interactive Research and the Research Contract

Coming back to the initial phase of our study, i e establishing access to the company and to the CEO as a person, that part was fairly easy. He was known to one of us beforehand. Furthermore, he took a lively interest in research with the main argument that he expected to learn new things. His job as a manager seldom offered him the time to read books. One should also remember that he was hired to renew the company and a study of renewal could be seen as supportive of that activity. He most likely also saw us as actors on the scene set up by him to perform his duties. Anyway, it was easy for us to form an implicit contract with regard to our mutual expectations concerning our work in the study.

Our initial introduction at the headquarters level of the company was stalled though. When the CEO brought the matter of the study to the executive group at a meeting where another matter of discussion was his initiative to create a new organizational unit, a staff unit, for technical development and consultancy, the reactions from the executive group were very negative. They in principle vetoed the new unit using various logical arguments, but on the implicit grounds that the unit would unduly increase powers of headquarters and decrease freedom of action at the subsidiaries. Furthermore, they expressed very negative views about initiating a research project at the time in question. Thus, the CEO concluded that we had to postpone the empirical phase of the study even though he himself was very much in favor of initiating the research effort as soon as possible. This sequence of events illustrates how the study at an early stage had become something of a hot issue within the organization, something in the minds of the executive group and something they had been relating to by taking a negative stand.

Several months later we were able to start our empirical work, but now the task was defined somewhat differently for the organizational members when we came to interview them. It differed in the sense that we expressed a major interest in the development of the business over time. This approach was more in line with the Diös culture since the founder had been documenting the business in several publications over the years, expecially company involvement with major restoration work (like the cathedral of Uppsala) and important cultural buildings. Only very briefly did we discuss the recent development of the company focusing on the actions of the new CEO and plausible effects of those actions. That approach appeared to be useful since we established very good contacts with almost all important actors of the company. In this way, we secured future access and rapport. There were two exceptions though. One of our interviewees avoided to give us any information of value in the interview and the other one got uneasy about having "revealed too much" and asked us to have the tape after the interview.

The events of the initial phase of the study are important in several ways. Firstly, access was a sequential matter. Our discussion with the new CEO went fairly smoothly (details are left out since they are judged to be of less importance in the present context) and we had a working agreement with him, an implicit research contract outlining expectations concerning the study, and in fact through him also a formal agreement with the company guaranteeing access to the company as such. In the second phase when the CEO tried to establish the research effort at the company headquarters level the project was stalled. As researchers that is the way we came to think about it at the time. The reaction from the executive group was an obstacle that had to be overcome. Another way of viewing the same thing would have been to think of it in terms of a temporary research system. When the research effort became a hot issue in the organization and when the actors had a reason to relate to it, the research system in a way transformed from consisting of the initial three of us to include several of the most important actors of the company. The attitude towards the research effort was very much dictated by the attitude towards the new CEO. In the third phase, when the broad empirical work was started and the attitude of the executive group members appeared to have shifted the research system did not change. Perhaps the willingness to endure interviews was even dictated by curiosity. We might have been regarded as potential informants concerning the activities of the CEO. Anyway, the temporary research system, or more appropriately a border organization between the research community and the field had been established. The issue had left the group level - the inner circle of the temporary research system and reached the organizational level - the outer circle.

As explicated, the initial phase of the study was important to us in the sense that the research system transformed itself. At the same time, and that is the second point to be made, the system under research changed. The incident also marked a transformation in that relations between actors were established. People had to relate to the new CEO over the issue. The resistance could have been a sort of signal to the CEO that relations of "him and us" character were building. In retrospect you may say that the CEO failed to apply that subjective rationality. Rather he accepted the logical arguments presented by the resistance. And we did not inform him about the potential hazards of the situation either. Mostly because we did not perceive it that way quite clearly at the time, but partly also because responsibility for the research does not (necessarily) encompass full responsibilities for the organization under study. So, clearly the transformation of the research system involves important ethical considerations.

At a later stage of our work we learned that some of the people we talked to in our first round of interviews mistook us for two of the consultants that the new CEO had hired to do some work on the organization and on the economic system. At the interviews the possibilities of mistaken identity never occurred to us. This illustrates that researchers are possibly the least suitable to judge their own effects on the organization. The question of "who studies the student" thus is a suitable issue for the research contract.

Renegotiating the Contract and Exit

Any research project, but especially a naturalistic inquiry lives its own life in the sense that research questions and preliminary answers shift over time (cf Lincoln & Guba, 1985). In the present context, we leave those aspects of the temporary system metaphor out. Instead we concentrate on the crucial phases of a study like initiation, exit or fundamental change.

The case just described included one fundamental change when the October revolution was engineered. At that time not only did the stream of events change direction, but our main informant, the CEO was ousted, and our research contract with him became of limited value. Furthermore, since the new ownership had other plans for the company, almost contradictory to the strategy followed by the CEO, the renewal efforts now took a different turn. Going public and getting the company's shares listed on the stock market exchange was now the main overall strategy. Renewal in construction activities was considered less important not to say unimportant.

The October revolution came as a total surprise to us. During the spring of 1986, especially after mr Diös accidentally fell and broke his leg, we suspected that something of that kind might happen. Towards the end of the summer with improving business conditions and with the company picking up financial strength that suspicion had evaporated, though. And when the revolution occurred we were in fact approaching the summary phase of our studies, but now there were reasons for further interest. For that purpose we had to establish a contract with the new leaders. Fairly few people within the company seemed to have been involved with the revolution, though. Two of them belonged to the group interviewed by us, one of them a representative of the owners and the other one the board member, who was to become the CEO replacement. With the change of focus the study of course became of less importance for the new leadership cadre. However, we were given the opportunity to continue the study as we wished granted that the "going public" plans would not be hurt. A new implicit contract could be "signed" at the same time as our contract with the CEO who had been ousted was still valid with him as a person and we had all the opportunities we needed to work with him. The dual connections were helpful for us when we were trying to disentangle the October revolution, but the situation really was a stern test of our abilities to balance views since the new leadership lived out the need to downgrade the efforts of the previous CEO at the same time as he had been stigmatized by the revolution and felt a strong urge to plead his cause.

The final phase of our study was designed to find explanations to the revolution and to be a follow-up of the revolution itself. The easy part consisted of following the efforts of the company to go public. As to the mechanisms behind the revolution, that part turned out to be very tricky. Ethical considerations came to fore during the exit phase, especially since it turned out to be impossible to present findings and keeping the company name a secret. Due to the special circumstances the efforts to finalize the project were fairly lengthy. In retrospect we should have planned for a more project like research activity. Our experiences indicate that research work might gain from experiences from the project management approach at the conceptual level.

Research as Project Work

There appears to be an overall, general trend in management towards project management (cf Gareis, 1990), where managers to an increasing extent arrange their work in terms of projects. The total managerial task thus conceived consists of a portfolio of projects to be handled in parallel or in sequence. Ordinarily, a project in the managerial portfolio has certain characteristics (cf Christiansen & Kreiner, 1989) focusing the project as a task oriented way to organize work:

a) It is limited in time and scope (a predetermined termination point, a predetermined task and predetermined resources).
b) It has explicitly stated (or implicitly understood) and well defined goals.
c) It involves at least two persons, mostly several, one of whom acts as a leader (with clear-cut responsibilities, one of them being hand–ling project disturbances).
d) It presupposes information sharing between persons involved (open information).
e) It follows a rationalistic plan.
f) It is subject to an implicit or explicit evaluation in terms of objec–tives reached as part of the project.

In its traditional managerial conception, project work emphasizes most rationalistic and technocratic requirements like cost and time limitations of a project, quality specifications and the task to be completed. Lately emphasis has also been shifting to human aspects of project work (cf e g Briner et al, 1990) in terms of teamwork, commitment and worker satisfaction, even though the prototype from the construction industry still prevails in practice. However, one should take note that at the conceptual level a project involves a temporary system to accomplish a specific task. The role of management in such a context like e g in construction is not only to set up plans and to implement them, but also to handle situations, when disturbances occur. That very essential managerial task has been named "disturbance handling" (Mintzberg, 1973, pp 81 - 85). A disturbance is when something unforeseen happens that threatens to violate time or budget constraints. And the general experience is that in construction "unforeseen" disturbances always happen. A quite common saying in the construction industry is that "we know that disturbances will occur, but we do not know when or where".

In research projects work might be conceived of and handled in the same way as for any kind of project. An enumeration of the same type and like the general one above adapted to a research project might include the following general characteristics (please notice similarities and differences):

a) It is limited in time and partly in scope (the task is only partially predetermined and so are the resources).
b) It has an explicitely stated but possibly not very well defined goal.
c) It involves at least two persons, often several, one of whom is responsible for the research project and one or several of the others might be responsible for the system or the organization under study.
d) It presupposes information sharing (with some ethically motivated restrictions).
e) It follows a plan that is subject to change.
f) It is subject to disturbances that not only should be handled but their implications for the research edifice should be a matter of major concern.
g) It is evaluated from the practitioners and researchers both as part of the project and with an outside perspective.

Comparing the points a) through g) above with regular project work gives us an opportunity to scrutinize research as project work:

A) The limitations in time and scope are especially valid for funded research where time and cost limitations are part of the research deal. However, the research effort might gain from being pro–longed (cf the case just described).

B) The goals are certainly less well defined for research work, especially for naturalistic designs where generating theory rather than theory testing and applying what Agar calls "the received view of science" comes to the fore
(Agar, 1986, pp 11 - 13).

C) Responsibilities differ considerably for the participants. Not only does the outcome of research count, but for those sharing responsibilities for the system under study, i e real life action, research is only of secondary interest.

D) Information sharing is certainly desirable for the researcher(s), but not always attained due to differences in goals for the participants involved in the research activities.

E) Unforeseen events change focus for research to an extent that could never be accepted in a construction project. And in research projects more than in regular project work is it appears particu-larly important to consider what the disturbances are and what effects they have.

F) Interrupting a research project is more easily done than interrupting a project of the concrete type (like construction). Phrased differently, power in a research project is unevenly distributed.

In general, project characteristics of research work are more often than not disregarded. Most research projects are of course considerably more open than the construction prototype and there is more stress on the human experiences. Certainly, human aspects of studies of living systems as organizations are important for the researcher purporting to avoid bias by acting in an inconspicuous way (cf the reasoning in Lundin & Wirdenius, 1990). And when it comes to interactions with the main gatekeeper(s) it is our experience that it usually is worthwhile spending more effort than customary to forestall potential drawbacks in the future. To summarize, we want to highlight some crucial characteristics of a research project - a temporary reserach system - as it develops over time.

Access, Disturbances and Exit in Interactive Research

The initial access phase involves locating main gatekeepers of the organization, getting an initial aquaintance with the organization in terms of relations between main gatekeepers and getting to know them. Initial access also involves establishing points of mutual interest for the researchers and the company people, formulating a preliminary picture of the crucial system for interaction and setting up the preliminary research contract embodying the inner circle of the temporary research system. An important question in this phase centers on possibilities to find common interests and unite expectation for the parties involved. Is it possible for practitioners and researchers to unite within the research endeavour? Reasons for easy access as well as problematic access are worthy of consideration (cf Burgess, 1984). One should also remember that research generates focus in a general overload situation. Understanding the behavior of the temporary system also has a bearing upon final analysis and synthesis.

As soon as a research project has been initiated empirically, the researcher looses some of the control. The project becomes part of "real life" and thus susceptible to disturbances. Disturbances to look out for in interactive research could be operationally defined as when emotions among people in the temporary research system are stirred. Some emotions you can foresee using information from internal and external sources. Disturbances that you did not foresee might involve important clues concerning hidden mechanisms. The October revolution as described in the case involved a disturbance occurring in the outer circle of the temporary research system even though the inner circle was also affected.

The researcher should also be on guard concerning her own reactions. A researcher can never be a dispassionate of the world (cf Susman, 1983). Anyway, encounters with disturbances should be reported as part of the findings, since disturbances viewed with focus on the researcher involve events that might give clues to other researchers (cf Alvesson, 1989, pp 58 - 61).

Exit in interactive research involves not only terminating efforts but more importantly, ethical considerations. The exit part of a study also involves analysis and there is a possibility to involve practitioners in the analysis (participatory analysis) further stressing interactive aspects (cf Philips, 1988, pp 60 - 63), since we all certainly want our research to encompass an AHA experience for the practitioners involved. Thus, we should always be aware of the fact the exit is less of a decisive bracket when compared with entry (or access). Leaving the field and communicating findings involves emotions for the researcher

(Jorgensen, 1989, pp 117 - 123). And leaving also involves something of a final distancing effort on the part of the researcher (Solberg, 1982). It has even been suggested that in order to make it possible for the researcher to exit, the matter of the termination date should explicitly be settled in the research contract (Jönsson, 1990). However, the possibility to revisit the research site might be of special interest to the researcher. Revisiting implies that actors have had a chance to distance themselves from the inquiry in question so that a more relaxed form of rapport can be secured. To put the whole reasoning in different words, a temporary research system is not easily dissolved.

References

Agar, M. H., (1986), Speaking of Ethnography, Beverly Hills, CA: SAGE.

Alvesson, M., (1989), Ledning av kunskapsföretag, (Managing Know- How Companies), Stockholm, Sweden: Norstedts.

Argyris, C. and Schön, D.A., (1991), Participatory Action Research and Action Science Compared, In William Foot Whyte (ed.): Participatory Action Research, Newbury Park, CA: SAGE, pp 85 - 96.

Briner, W., Geddes, M. and Hastings C., (1990), Project Leadership Aldershot, Hants, England: Gower.

Burgess, R. G., (1984), In the Field. An Introduction to Field Research. London, England: Unwin Hyman.

Christensen, S. and Kreiner K., (1989), Projektledelse i en ufuldkommen verden (Project Management in an Imperfect World), Ökonomi-styring & Informatik (Economic Control and Informatics), Vol 5 no 2, pp 113 - 130.

Gareis, R. (ed.), (1990), Handbook of Management by Projects, Vienna, Austria: MANZ.

Jorgensen, D. L., (1989), Participant Observation - A Methodology for Human Studies, Beverly Hills, CA: SAGE.

Jönsson, S., (1990), Action Research. Paper presented at the IFIP conference on "The Information Systems Research Arena of the 90's", Copenhagen, Denmark (December 14 - 16).

Lewin, K., (1951), Field Theory in Social Science, New York: Harper.

Lincoln, Y. S. and Egon G. G., (1985), Naturalistic Inquiry, Beverly Hills, CA: SAGE.

Lundin, R. A. and Wirdenius H., (1989), Företagsförnyelse och kultur–skifte - Erfarenheter från Diös-koncernen (Enterprise Renewal and Cultural Change - Experiences from the Diös Group), Stockholm, Sweden: Norstedts.

Lundin, R. A. and Wirdenius H., (1990), Interactive Research, Scandi–navian Journal of Management, Vol 6 no 2, pp 124 - 142.

Marshall, C. and Rossman G. B., (1989), Designing Qualitative Research, Beverly Hills, CA: SAGE.

Mintzberg, H., (1973), The Nature of Managerial Work, New York: Harper & Row.

Philips, Å., (1988), Eldsjälar, En studie av aktörsskap i arbetsorganisa–toriskt utvecklingsarbete (Souls of Fire. A Study of Actorship in Work Organization Development Effort), Stockholm: Ekono–miska forskningsinstitutet, Handelshögskolan i Stockholm.

Reeves Sanday, P., (1983), The ethnographic paradigm, In John Van Maanen (ed.): Qualitative Methodology, Beverly Hills, CA: SAGE, pp 19 - 36.

Solberg, A., (1982), Erfaringer fra feltarbeid (Experiences from Field Work). In: Harriet Holter and Ragnvald Kalleberg (eds.): Kvalitative metoder i samfunnsforskning (Qualitative Methods in the Social Sciences), Oslo, Norway: Universitetsforlaget, pp 123 - 136.

Susman, G. I., (1983), Action research: A sociotechnical systems perspective. In: Morgan G. (ed.): Beyond Method - Strategies for Social Research, Beverly Hills, CA: SAGE, pp 95 - 113.

Part 3

Outlining Networks of Restrictions and Social Interaction

INNOVATION VS. CONTROL IN A LOCAL INFORMATION SYSTEMS ENVIRONMENT[*]

Salvador Carmona
Isabel Gutierrez
Universidad Carlos III - Universidad de Sevilla

Introduction

The management of operations in highly competitive sectors requires simultaneous activity in the areas of quality, delivery time and cost. Strategies of differentiation or costs by themselves only provide a partial view of a much more complex competitive environment. Consequently, competition develops parallelly in costs and differentiation (Porter, 1980), acquiring a three-dimensional character that can be represented in the following form;

Figure 1. Elements of a competitive environment

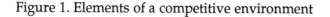

[*] The authors would like to acknowledge the financial support of the grant PB 0622/89 of the Spanish Agency for Science and Technology (DGCYT) and the comments of Jill Arcaro which improved the English version of this paper.

97

Currently, these three variables must be taken into consideration during the phase of production design as well as during the daily management of production. The former requires continuous innovation in new technologies while the latter requires continuous improvement on the shop floor. The first stage develops basically at the central level of organization whilst the second does so at the local level. Jönsson and Grönlund (1988) proposed the basis of some information systems (local information systems) that would make organizational learning in activities like those synthesized in Graph 1, easier at a lower organizational level. Jönsson and Grönlund's theoretical and empirical development identifies the lowest organizational level, or operating core (Mintzberg, 1979), at the local level. The restrictive character of this definition poses a question about the possibility of designing and implementing a Local Information System (LIS) at other organizational levels.

The aim of this paper is to analyze the conditions that are required to design and implement a Local Information System in order to examine its flexibility for development at different organizational levels.

The empirical experience that supports this paper stems from a long-term project which took place at the Spanish subsidiary of an important multinational firm in the automobile sector. For confidential reasons, we shall call this firm OMEGA here. The experience was gained during the active participation in the design and implementation of a Local Information System in this organization.

Theoretical Foundations of Local Information Systems

Jönsson and Grönlund (1988: 522) sum up the requirements that a Local Information System must fulfill in the three following points:

- Different types of control are found on different levels of an organization; lower levels that are more operative than higher ones relying more on behavioral control.

- There are also different kinds of learning on different levels. On lower levels learning is likely to be experiential and based on direct observation of processes, while the integrative and coordinative levels are more likely to use structuralist learning based on conceptual models.

- Finally, hard data are likely to be used in "stewardship" situations while soft data are more prevalent in learning situations where new frames of reference are built on cost improvement experiments (emphasis supplied).

Organizational Setting

OMEGA was founded at the beginning of the 1980's. Its initial strategy foresaw the manufacturing of one basic component for the automobile that would be sold to European firms, both belonging to the multinational group and detached from it. The organizational objective was "customer satisfaction" but in regard to its initial strategy, it was unable to comply with the product specifications of firms outside the multinational group because of lengthly learning processes and inflexible installations. This resulted in OMEGA manufacturing at this beginning stage, only for allied firms. As soon as learning processes were mastered and the uncertainty of manufacturing processes were reduced, managers from the home office began to be substituted for Spanish executives. The substitution period coincided with the decision to adopt the initial strategy of sales to clients outside the multinational group. This decision made necessary additional investments in order to achieve a certain flexibility in the production plant by installing production processes which incorporated advanced technologies. Additional investments were needed for the creation of a Sales Department and of a Research and Development Department.

In the fall of 1987 the first contracts were signed with outside firms. The sales plan stipulated that these orders would be delivered in the beginning of the summer 1988 or in 1989. The experience referred to in this research paper deals with the period between January - September, 1988.

Who Are The Clients ?

As we have already said, the firm's aim is customer satisfaction and for this reason, many external conditions are going to considerably affect its organization, especially its information system. This section analyzes the firm's relationship with these external conditions during the period in which it changed its strategy.

In 1985, OMEGA had consolidated its learning processes on the shop floor. This fact, along with the stabilization in the volume of orders guaranteed by allied companies, framed a situation in which uncertainty for the most part, was not due to the market or technology. Even though customer satisfaction is OMEGA's goal, the concept of client actually becomes relative if his needs do not generate any uncertainty. In this context, the greatest source of uncertainty came from the home office that provided OMEGA with a considerable amount of resources: financing, technology, top executives and even, orders from allied firms. So, the final objective that OMEGA had was the satisfaction of requirement coming from its home office, its' "client". In relation to OMEGA the home office recognized a strong environment (Mellemvik et al, 1988) which required legitimation. The process of legitimation was articulated through the budgetary system.

Nevertheless, from the moment in which contracts were obtained with customers outside the group, a substantial change is produced within OMEGA's environment. OMEGA's dependence on the home office is reduced with its diversification outside the group of up to 30% of all sales. Opposed to its relationship with allied customers which was indirect through the home office, OMEGA's business relations with these new customers are bilateral. Inherent in this bilateralism is the responsibility of management and in order to achieve the aim of customer satisfaction, they will have to deal with a large amount of technological and market uncertainty. In this new setting the customer's quality, price/cost and delivery requirements, seen in Graph 1, will be of prime importance.

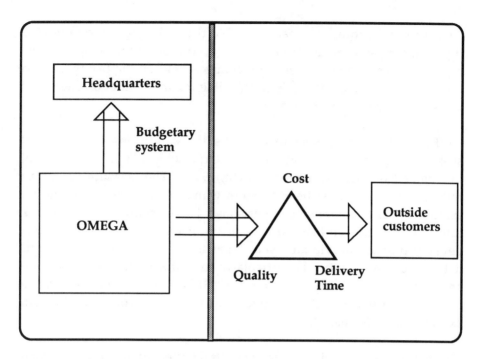

Figure 2 . The process of legitimation

The Central Information System

In each one of these two stages, before and after obtaining contracts with outside customers, OMEGA's informational needs were substantially different. In the following two sections we shall analyze characteristics of the information system in so far as its design and implementation into the firm.

OMEGA belongs to a multinational corporation with a sophisticated budgetary procedure. The control of the budget is carried out during a monthly meeting with the home office's directorial staff. The budget is an important source of bureaucracy within the organization and the number of documents which budgetary control generates is so great that one of OMEGA's managers commented, "we seem like a publishing firm". One sheet synthesizes 33 key variables that must be reported and that basically refer to personnel, materials, quality, maintenance, overhead and profit. For each variable the real figure, the budgeted figure and a figure taken from an advanced monthly forecast must be reported. The budgetary control meeting is held on the telephone and each of OMEGA's directors is responsible for the results of one set of variables which he/she reports orally.

OMEGA's budgetary system contains the conditions for a central system of information (Jönsson and Grönlund, 1988). The control maintained is output-oriented (Ouchi, 1978): The measure of output reflects precisely what headquarters wants to take place, including standard data to establish comparisons. The measures of output lack causal information and support a structuralist learning theory which is developed at an individual level. Likewise, the data reported is hard data. Budgetary control is particularly strict during the period we are analyzing here (January-September, 1988) because it coincides with a desire to emphasize control over the recently appointed Spanish executive's performance.

The budgetary system is an efficient central system of information which satisfies OMEGA's need to please its "customer", the home office. Besides introducing a rational element in its organization and fulfilling the functions of code, channel and standard (Walsh and Dewar, 1987). The budget as code reduces a complex set of activities to relatively less complex formulae. The budget as channel formalizates routes and prohibits others, thus makes interaction predictable. And finally, as standard, the budget establishes the measures against which the actions are compared and rewards or punishments are given out.

However, the system is not enough to deal with the uncertainty that is generated on the shop floor by the manufacturing of products with different characteristics and technologies. As observed, rationalization is the typical response to complexity. An apparent difficulty with ratio-nalization, however, is that when a once stable environment becomes more uncertain the organization seems to have difficulties deratio-nalizing, that is, removing rules and procedures and relying more on individual discretion in order to become more adaptative (Lee, 1984).

The Local Information System

A year and a half before the mass manufacturing of new products, OMEGA's management understood that to assure the satisfaction of new customers, continual improvements on new manufacturing processes were needed. The information required to support these improvements was at that time missing or scattered.

Jönsson and Grönlund (1988) analyze the differences between the local system and the central system identifying them on two different hierarchical levels. The local system is seen at the lowest level of organization and the central system at higher hierarchical levels. However, the main characteristic of the local system is not found in the low hierarchical level of its geographical location. On the contrary, the root of the local system is its support in the process of decision making and not in the process of control as can be deduced from the characteristics discussed in Section 2. In other words, the essence of the local system is found in its contribution to the generation of activities, not bureaucracy. OMEGA's management understood that this Local Information System would fulfill their new informative needs because they were aware that their current organizational structure only permitted a sufficient degree of autonomy at OMEGA's highest hierarchical level.

The informative needs of OMEGA at the beginning of 1988 were very similar in their content to the needs of the teams involved in the Jönsson and Grönlund pilot project: an information system differing and independent from the central one, supportive to the decision making process, generating activities and introducing innovation.

The success of an information system depends on the confidence which exists between its user and its designer (Khadwalla, 1972). For this reason, various meeting were needed until the confidence of the firm's researcher could be won. The Local Information System project counted on the active participation of the firm's researcher in its design and implementation so that the impact of the new information system on organization could be analyzed (Hopwood, 1978).

There were two restrictions to the design of a local information system: a) the system in action must not create more bureaucracy at OMEGA, b) the directors' overload of work and consequently, their limited capacity to process information, required that the Local Information System consist of a limited number of variables.

On the other hand, there were various objectives that the Local Information System needed to meet: a) to make organizational learning easier, for which it must have a semi-confusing character (Hedberg and Jönsson, 1978), facilitating interchange of ideas between members of the directorial staff, b) be a long-term project with no set goals which would end the cooperation among directives once met, but rather it should enhance innovation through interaction, c) to facilitate the firm's adaptation to a continually more complex work setting in the future.

After several meetings between the directives and the team formed by the Finance Department and the researcher, a system of information was proposed based on two variables: quality and leadtime. These two variables can be found in two vertexes of the triangle illustrating operational priorities in Graph 1. The third dimension (cost) was thoroughly controlled by the budgetary system. The variable of quality is developed as in the cost of quality classification proposed by Juran and Gryna (1980): prevention costs, inspection, internal and external errors. The analysis of leadtime would not include value added activities and would eliminate idle activities like waiting time for materials, movement time, set up time, etc.

This proposal for an information system was approved by OMEGA's directors in July, 1988.

The Implementation of The Local Information System

Spanish mentality encouraged simultaneously performing various actions in order to take advantage of the director's initial enthusiasm. This was a different focus than that proposed by Jönsson and Grönlund who recommended carrying out just one action at a time.

The fact that this Local Information System did not require additional work in collecting information made rapid use of it much easier. Nevertheless, during the decision making process members of the directorial staff were reluctant to make decisions which would raise the amount budgeted for their respective departments in 1988. This is to say that their behavior was mainly orientated by their interest in adhering to the budgetary system instead of in using the Local Information System. The budget controlled the directorial staff's behavior by controlling output.

For example, an action tending to reduce the leadtime by improving the handling of materials but which required a training course was evaluated positively. However, the decision to implement it was never agreed upon because of the disagreement amongst the departments to assume the training costs.

In reality the strict budgetary control of the home office acted as a stabilizing element within the organization. The top managers refused to make a decision in order to win a competitive advantage the results of which would become clear a year later if that, in the meantime, put in disadvantage their monthly reports to headquarters. On a short term, budgetary control acted as a temporary map for decisions and conditioned its users to acting always on a short term basis. In contrast, the Local Information System was designed to encourage the anticipated learning of activities which would be developed later on. In summary, the failure in the implementation of this Local Information System is due to a conflict between the rigid structure of control (represented by the budget), which eased social reproduction, and an innovative element (represented by the Local Information System), which eased social change (Giddens, 1984).

Conclusions

A Local Information System is not a geographical concept only valid at low organizational levels. On the contrary, the local system is based on an element for the programming of innovation through the generation of activities and the development of organizational learning. These activities do not belong solely at the lowest organizational levels.

In OMEGA's case a Local Information System at the highest level of organization united the design characteristics mentioned by Jönsson and Grönlund (1988). However, being an information system which pretended to contribute to the development of organizational learning and not individual learning, the Local Information System required special conditions to implement it. In summation, its implementation requires the organization's positive attitude toward innovation and change. Here a conflict between stabilizing elements within the organization, represented by the budgetary system and elements proposing social change, represented by the Local Information System, were verified. In OMEGA's case, this conflict conditioned the effectiveness of the Local Information System.

N.B.: In the spring of 1990 the home office asked for a quarterly report covering: quality cost and leadtime - the very two variables which the Local Information System proposed two years earlier contained. The results have been spectacular.

References

Carmona, S., (1990), Aspectos contables y economico-financieros de la gestion de operaciones (The impact of Modern Operations Management on Accounting), Revista de Economia, 7.

Giddens, A., (1984), The Constitution of Society, Oxford: Polity Press.

Hedberg, B. and Jönsson, S., (1984), Designing Semi-Confusing Information Systems for Organizations in Changing Environments, Accounting, Organizations and Society, pp 47-64.

Hopwood, A., (1978), Editorial, Accounting, Organizations and Society, pp 93-95.

Jönsson, S. and Grönlund, A., (1988), Life with a Sub-Contractor: New Technology and Management Accounting, <u>Accounting, Organizations and Society</u>, Vol 13, No 5, pp 512-532.

Juran, J. M. and Gryna F. M., (1980), Quality Planning and Analysis, New York: McGraw Hill, 2nd Edition.

Khandwalla, P. N., (1972), The Effect of Different Type of Competition on the Use of Management Controls, <u>Journal of Accounting Research</u>, Autumn, pp 275-285.

Mellemvik, F., Monsen N., Olson O., (1988), The Functions of Accounting, <u>The Scandinavian Journal of Management</u>, pp 101-119.

Mintzberg, H., (1979), The Structuring of Organizations, Englewood Cliffs: Prentice Hall.

Ouchi, W., (1978), The Relationship between Organizational Structure and Organizational Control, <u>The Administrative Science Quarterly</u>, p 95.

Porter, M., (1980), Competitive Strategy, New York: The Free Press.

Walsh, J. P., and Dewar, R., (1987), Formalization and the Organizational Life Cycle, <u>Journal of Management Studies</u>, Vol 24, 3, 1987, pp 215-231.

INTERNAL PRICES BASED ON NEGOTIATION IN RELATION TO ORGANIZATIONAL PROCESSES AND STRUCTURES

Olof Arwidi
Lund University

In Scandinavia, Sten Jönsson has been a pioneer in the study of accounting in relation to organizational structures and processes. This article is based on ideas which have been inspired by the tradition represented by Sten Jönsson, where technical instruments and system structures are components in an organizational context. In this context, "talk" and conflicts may be just as crucial forces in achieving organizational success as rational models.

This article starts with a discussion based on the literature of internal pricing with an emphasis on the various functions of internal prices in conjunction with structure and process. Special attention is paid to the situation associated with the chief focus of this article, namely the determination of internal prices between dependent units in an organization, with limited opportunities for choice as suppliers or buyers in a given situation and with no external prices which are directly comparable.

The second section deals with the problem of internal pricing in a specific organization - firstly on the basis of certain observations at a specific point in time and subsequently on the basis of how the prerequisites change.

The article is summarized in the form of some final reflections and conclusions.

Some observations based on the literature in the field

From a conceptual point of view, a distinction is often drawn between internal prices based on costs and internal prices based on the market price. An alternative starting point is to take structural prerequisites as a basis for the selection and design of internal price models, where the price determination process is seen as part of the solution in an organizational context.

Negotiated Internal Prices - a Hybrid

Vancil's classic study of "Decentralisation: Managerial Ambiguity by Design" (1978) contains a schedule which lists how internal prices are employed in practice. Vancil indicates that negotiation-based internal prices are used in more than 20 % of the cases. His list starts with various cost-based models, continues to run through market-based models and winds up with negotiation-based variants. Both Vancil's classification and the percentage figure he quotes for negotiation-based prices may merit attention and be worth questioning.

In his book, "Advanced Management Accounting" (1982), Kaplan is dissatisfied with the high proportion (45 %) of models based on full-cost price. He sees no logical basis for this phenomenon, but he does feel that it is encouraging that more than 50 % of companies employ market-based prices, including prices based on negotiation. A number of earlier questionnaires in the US and Britain have certainly indicated that negotiation-based internal prices have been stated to be around 20 %, but they are then normally associated with cost-based models. A survey emanating from Price Waterhouse (1984), based on 74 of the 150 largest US companies, indicates that in almost 80 % of the cases where cost-based pricing was employed, negotiation-based pricing also formed part of the picture. These observations are more in line with the observations made in other contexts (e g Arvidsson (1971) and Tomkins (1990)) which indicate that internal pricing with negotiation normally takes place in a situation where cost-based prices with a mark-up are employed. Tomkins even goes so far as to question whether there is really any cost-based internal pricing without some form of discussion or "managerial adjustment" when the situation invites such behaviour and where this can occur without the knowledge of the central unit in the company. On the other hand, there are authors (e g Hansson and Skärvad (1986)) who maintain that negotiation-based internal pricing is not particularly common.

We may wonder whether conceptualisation of negotiation-based internal prices as market-based or cost-based is relevant. And we may also ask how relevant it is to indicate, on the basis of questionnaires, a percentage of occasions where negotiated prices are employed, if the meaning of the concept is fluid. Perhaps, instead, the fact is that negotiation-based pricing cannot be unambiguously classified either as **market-based or cost-based**, and that it is not meaningful to separate negotiation processes **from the organizational context** in which these classifications are used.

Let us start by recapitulating some of the basic information we have about internal pricing.

Focus on Models and Situations

The pricing of internal performances has a long history (Frenckner (1954)), but the American debate really started in 1955 after the publication of two articles with almost identical titles: Cook's "Decentralisation and the Transfer Price Problem" and Dean's "Decentralisation and Intracompany Pricing". Both authors assumed that internal prices would be set on the basis of estimates of the market price.

These articles led to the initiation of a debate on the prerequisites for the utilization of various pricing models. Hirshleifer's (1956 and 1957) contributions, which were based on economic theory, were important in this context. Hirshleifer employed marginal analysis to attack the problem and he established where the market price could be used directly and where marginal cost ought to be applied. This can be seen as the starting point for two different approaches.

One approach came to base itself on mathematical models, built on various assumptions about the economic prerequisites. Subsequently, this approach was heavily criticized both by organizationally oriented researchers and by scholars who combined model approaches with empirical work. Thus, Verlage (1975) and Abdel-Khalik and Lusk (1974) focused their criticism on the prerequisites for the models. Watson and Baumler (1976), on the other hand, criticized the organizational perspective which characterized these constructions, while Kaplan (1982) criticized both the conditions for the models and their organizational implications. In addition, it may be commented that mathematical models such as linear programming have hardly had any impact in practice.

A much more important further development of this debate from a practical point of view lay in various kinds of typology for the sort of internal pricing model which was supposed to be most appropriate under specific organizational and market circumstances. A classification of this kind, which is almost classic, can be found in Solomons (1965, pp 198-205), where situations are categorized under five main headings, including a discussion of viable internal price models in relation to the situation in question. This approach is the dominant feature of many books in the management accounting area which discuss the question of internal pricing. Antony and Dearden's "Management Control Systems" (various editions 1965-1989) and Kaplan and Atkinson's "Advanced Management Accounting" (1989) are two typical examples which discuss and analyse which internal price model is "best", given certain organizational and market conditions. A mixture of deduction and discussion, based on practical observation is often employed in this context. Arvidsson's "Internpriser" (1971) may be said to represent a Swedish - and empirically oriented - equivalent. The focus here is on analysis of the conditions for employing a given type of model and, by and large, this approach may be classified as structural.

Process and Function Rather than Method

Dean (1955) regarded negotiation as a means of determining price (amongst other things as an expression of market competition).

Although we may note that these early writers were not unaware of negotiation as a process, their goal was to achieve "efficient" decision-making. One example was the difference of opinion between Dearden (1960) and Dean (1955) regarding central management's possibilities of intervening and influencing the pricing decision. Dearden, in contrast to Dean, recommended intervention as a method for the avoidance of "constant quarrelling" and for the coordination of decision-making. Shillinglaw (1977) also distinguished between the method selected and the process for determination, where he saw one of the reasons for negotiation as the assessment of the internal prices as "fair" by managers with divisional responsibility. Since this is a subjective quality, Shillinglaw considered it was important to be able to "test and verify the price by means of market transaction". By including the criterion of "fair", he gave negotiation a special dimension which also meant that he formulated four different conditions for negotiation-based internal prices which meant, in principle, that the parties involved were to have the freedom to exploit external markets (p 859). On the other hand, no special function was indicated for negotiations.

Watson and Baumler (1976), in contrast, gave negotiation a special function. They regarded predetermined models for internal pricing, particularly mathematical programming models as having their major area of application when organizational units are relatively independent and when conditions are relatively stable. They observed that **internal prices** have a **function in differentiating** different organizational units from each other because they are given separate responsibility for results, but also that this leads to a need for coordination between these different units. Thus, one of the main points made by Watson and Baumler was that **negotiation has an intermediary integrative function**. By asserting the organizational perspective, the point was made that, on the one hand the internal price must be seen in relation to structural prerequisites in the environment and, on the other hand, that the negotiation process itself can be employed to facilitate communication between the various units to support the integration of the functions. Thus, the internal price system itself has the purpose of dividing up (differentiating) the organization into different profit centers, while the process of determination can be employed to coordinate (integrate) the various organizational units.

Organizational structure is of crucial importance in Eccles' work on "The Transfer Pricing System" (1985), which was subtitled "A Theory for Practice". Eccles distinguished between a number of different situations which were based both on the company's strategy and on the external prerequisites. Eccles was primarily interested in considering how corporate management can handle internal prices in such situations. A major basis for categorization was the typology the company uses to integrate the different corporate units. If companies employ a vertical strategy with mandatory cohesion between purchasing and sales units, internal prices will not determine the sourcing of the goods which are traded but will primarily be used to distinguish between the various units from a profit's/result's point of view.

Eccles demonstrated here that both the structure within which prices are established and the process under which prices are determined are worthy of study. In a situation with an explicit vertical strategy and a manadatory buy/sell situation, dependence on resources and inter-dependence between the units will be marked. In a situation of this kind, negotiations and communication will be relatively more important, and this will lead to conflicts as a natural result of internal price determination. In fact, the internal price is a decisive factor for the pro-fits of the different corporate units, while at the same time alternative potential solutions have been limited in quantity terms. Both integration between and the opportunities for evaluation beyond the limits of corporate units will then be particularly important in this context.

In an article entitled "Transfer Pricing Under Bilateral Bargaining", Chalos and Haka (1990) dealt experimentally with the situation where profits from buying and selling are made dependent on internal price negotiations. Rewards for the units and certainty in assessing various market alternatives change in the course of the experiment. The experiment applied to both single-period and multi-period negotiations. One interesting result of the experiment was that total corporate profits increased in a multi-period situation where learning effects were possible. The study also indicated that there are problems in determining rewards for the various units' separate profit tallies. It also showed that negotiation-based internal prices in a decentralized environment do not necessarily lead to profit maximization for the company or comparable evaluation of divisional achievements.

In another article published in 1990, Tomkins showed that negotiation-based internal prices which are based on cost prices should generally lead to results which do not deviate excessively from short-term profit maximization, if negotiations are conducted in a fairly reasonable manner and not too rigidly. Tomkins employed an analytical model. Apart from combining this analytical model with certain behavioural assumptions, Tomkins drew attention to a particularly important aspect of internal pricing: the multinational factor, where both the supplying and the buying units must produce profits, at least externally, so as to satisfy external requirements, for example the tax authorities. If there are no market prices, the mark-up based cost calculation becomes especially important in this context.

To summarize, this survey of the literature indicates that internal price negotiations fulfil integrative functions and that negotiations are particularly important if there are appreciable dependency relationships between organizational units. One such situation is vertical integration between buying and selling units which are unable to buy or sell in external markets. Price negotiations acquire crucial importance here, especially where the products are unique and there are no chances of making market comparisons. In such cases, there is no guarantee that such systems will lead to corporate profit maximization and therefore it will be particularly important that such systems and the environmental system are designed in a way which permits learning. In addition, it has been shown that in a situation where points of reference with comparable products on the market are lacking, cost price models with a mark-up are usually employed and that effects on corporate profits depend on the manner in which such models are used.

An illustration of negotiated internal prices in a vertically integrated international company

This illustration, or case study, has two main aims in the relation to the previous discussion. Firstly, to show on the basis of a study conducted at a specific point in time that internal prices are imbedded in a system where the structure and the process of determining prices have certain definite functions and, secondly, to indicate, on the basis of developments in a company, that although internal prices have not been structurally changed it is possible to achieve effects in the organization by changing the prerequisites for their application.

The first study was conducted in 1976 as a result of an enquiry from the company in question. The company's intention was not to achieve a tailor-made solution, but rather to gain an input for a conference which involved the participation of the managers of the various major subsidiaries (some 30 of them) and which would thus contribute to the company's own solution of its problems. The company received an intitial report which was translated into English and, prior to the conference, a presentation of the report was filmed in English for documentation purposes. Some time later, this study was produced in an anonymous form as a case study (Arwidi, 1977) and was presented as a brief research report entitled "Internal Pricing - as a Component in an Organizational System" ("Internprissättning - perspektivet komponent i ett organisationellt system") (Arwidi and Winquist, 1977).

The Company, the Product and the Markets

The company operates on an international scale and has thousands of employees in some 70 countries. The products which it manufactures are technically complex and demand considerable development, assembly know-how and service in local markets. The corporate group was divided into various divisons with different categories of products. The divisions were responsible for example for central production and central development and also for coordination between different activities in the product area. As a result of its geographical coverage, coordination in the corporate group was complex since each product divison operated in a network of up to 70 subsidiaries which were responsible for direct sales activities and contacts with customers, for example in assembly and sometimes even in manufacturing. Vertical integration meant that the product divisions only supplied to subsidiaries and that the subsidiaries largely worked with the products

116

supplied by the various product divisions. It was not really possible to purchase competitors' products.

Within the product division in question, the company was one of the world's leading manufacturers in its field. Broadly speaking, there were about half a dozen competitors. Direct price comparisons were hardly possible since competition took the form of a combination of technical applications, price, quality, service, etc.

The control system in which internal prices operated was characterized by a relatively far-reaching decentralization into investment and profit centers. This meant that all units were in principle evaluated by applying measures such as rate of return, etc. In addition, of course, there were estimates of market shares and other qualitatively-oriented criteria.

Top management was responsible for coordinated planning, evaluation and the development of central reporting systems.

It may be added that the organization was complicated by the breakdown of the subsidiaries sales function by customer industry - for example engineering, chemicals, foodstuffs, etc. Thus the organization was characterized by matrix-like dependency relationships. On the other hand, financial reporting took place on the basis of the various legally separate subsidiaries and the product divisions.

The products in the division which was studied may be characterized as technically complicated and of varying dimension, with some products which might be ten times more expensive than smaller models. The company's goals included the development of superior technical competence and the mastery of applications within a given number of defined key areas.

The Internal Pricing System

The calculations which provided a basis for internal prices may be regarded as technically comprehensive, but fundamentally relatively clearly structured. In principle, the calculation on which internal prices were based took place in two stages. Firstly, there was a manufacturing calculation which covered all the costs involved in production, including depreciation and interest on capital. This calculation was based on a standard computation. Before the products were priced from the product division to the sales companies, three types of mark-up were usually employed. Firstly, there was the product division's development costs, then there were the product division's joint costs and finally the product division's profit mark-up. The product of the standard computation and the various mark-ups constituted the basis for internal prices. Taking these prices as a starting point, the various subsidiaries then negotiated various discount rates on an individual basis. It should be noted in this context that these discount percentages covered the full range of products supplied by the product division to the subsidiary and that they might vary from zero to 20 % of the origin price (in extreme cases).

Negotiations on price took place once a year and were normally in the form of personal contacts (at least in the case of the major subsidiaries), where the subsidiary managers discussed price and other questions with product division managers. The result of these negotiations was the determination of discount rates for the subsidiary in question. The principles for calculation employed within the parent company were available to both the product division and the subsidiaries, and this also applied to the main cost items. On the other hand, the product division did not supply any information about discounts to the other subsidiaries. Instead, the product division surrounded the "book of prices" which contained the discount rates for the various subsidiaries with some secrecy.

Central group management was excluded from these price negotiations. If the product division and the subsidiary considered that they wanted to deviate from the standard price list and standard discount for strategic reasons, there was a further possibility - the limit price - which meant that a rebate was determined on the basis of a small precalculated mark-up on the manufacturing cost. There was then a breakdown of the surplus between the company's external price and the limit price on a shared basis between the product division and the sales company. This method was seldom employed, but it was an option to be used in exceptional circumstances.

The reason for the various differentiations based on the internal price as a result of negotiations and the use of the limit price was that there was a desire to maintain a certain degree of flexibility, depending on differences in competition and sales markets in different parts of the world. The subsidiaries relied on the margin between the purchase price for the product and the price they charged to their customers. This margin had to generate profits and cover the subsidiary's costs.

Effects of the Price Systems

On the basis of more general assumptions, it may be noted that linear internal prices mean greater profits for the supplier unit (the product division) as the volume increases. There is no corresponding position for sales units, since their cost and revenue functions are dependent on specific demand and cost conditions.

The generalised theoretical assumption that internal prices based on the cost price with mark-ups do not guarantee optimal behaviour for the whole system thus applies in this case too. It might also be noted that certain subsidiaries deliberately refrained from purchasing certain items in the product division's range since their profits were primarily generated by goods from other product divisions.

It might also be observed that subsidiaries which operated under relatively similar conditions could function with considerable differences in their price policies vis-a-vis their customers. This denoted that there was a relatively high degree of decentralization in the corporate group within the limits established by profit requirements. In one subsidiary, for example, significant rationalization measures were implemented, with a reduction in the volume of sales, and this led to an increased rate of return.

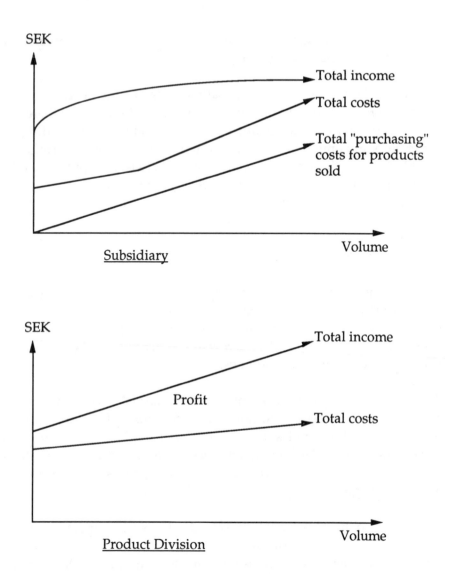

Figure 1. Effects of Linear Internal Prices - Illustration

It was also possible to perceive certain differences which were hard to explain logically. For example there were subsidiaries which worked under relatively similar structural conditions but with major differences in discount percentages and there were subsidiaries which had relatively high discounts, but which also had high customer prices. Furthermore there were examples of subsidiaries which had high discounts and a high rate of return. There were also various anecdotes about the reasons why certain subsidiary managers succeeded in getting better discounts than others - for example as a result of the manager's background or the arguments he employed about importance of his market. Such anecdotes indicate that central management found it difficult to evaluate the effects of the internal price system in concrete, specific situations. In any case, the guidance provided by normative internal pricing literature is relatively limited in this context.

Two Alternative Interpretations of the Pricing Situation

Apart from a logical analysis of the construction of the pricing system, the report on the price situation also contained two alternative interpretations. These two alternatives are briefly presented in the following.

While the product division's pricing model was built on a cost-based model, the models which the marketing units employed as a basis for discussion were grounded in differing market conditions. The marketing arguments thus tended to be based on what results could be achieved with an estimated sales price, minus the costs incurred for the relevant sales (for example service costs).

Thus, in the negotiations which took place there was, on the one hand, a relatively well documented model for allocating costs, while, on the other hand, there were the marketing unit's arguments regarding what the market could stand. While the principles for calculating costs were relatively familiar and could be proved on the basis of cost calculations for specific products, the marketing unit's views were not as standardized, prepackaged or externalized. On the other hand, it was far from uncommon to find that the marketing companies could both re-fer to previous outcomes (e g in comparison with the budgets of previous years) and that they could calculate outcomes on the basis of future budgets and plans. This illustrates that, in the actual negotiations of price, there was an encounter between, on the one hand, a cost orientation which was expressed in precalculated internal prices for different product groups and, on the other hand, the individual

121

marketing company's arguments for its own specific circumstances. Once the cost-oriented system was dealt with in accordance with pre-conceived principles and with established principles for mark-ups, there was rarely the same precision in the calculations on which the marketing units based their arguments.

However, one of the central points in the price negotiations was that a transfer of information between the individual marketing units and the product division occurred. Thus, as a result of the information on which price negotiations were based and the price negotiations themselves, opportunities for making an overall assessment of the consequences of the price policy pursued usually increased. At the same time, the establishment of prices and the negotiation process affected both motivation and the possibilities of conflicts. Since this is a question of mutual dependence relationships, where price affects the profits of each unit, such conflicts can hardly be regarded an unnatural (cf Eccles).

In the situation which has been described in this company, it is thus not a question of pure cost-orientation in negotiation, but rather an example of how two different models meet, one of which is formalized. The interaction between these two models may be illustrated in price negotiations in the following diagram:

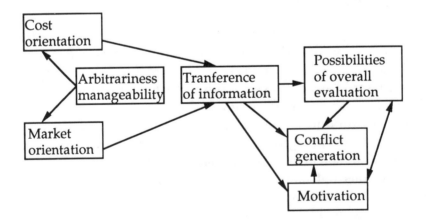

Figure 2. Cost-orientation and Market-orientation in Price
          Negotiations

Another interpretation of internal prices in an organizational context assumes that prices are only part of the control process. On the one hand, the rules for internal prices are supplemented by planning dialogues, while, on the other hand, the price system is supplemented by interpretation of results for the various units concerned. Genuine control of resource flows does not take place until planning dialogues and interpretation of results have taken place, and, in their turn, they give rise to product market behaviour. This approach to the problem of setting prices means that the prices are not in themselves regarded as having an exclusive role in controlling role for the prices and volumes which produce profits and results. Thus, this is a direct break with a tradition which is directly based on the calculation of effects under given circumstances (cf Hirsheifer).

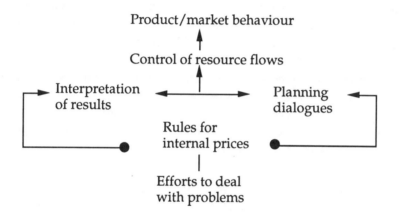

Figure 3. The Effects of Internal Price Systems

Assuming a starting point of this kind, neither the profit criteria nor the manner in which prices are determined is irrelevant for how the flow of resources is controlled and what effects this flow will have in terms of product market behaviour. For example, this means that if the success criteria for sales-oriented units are changed from rate of return measures to volume-oriented or margin-related measures, this will also have effects on the flow of resources and on product market behaviour. Similarly, with this starting point, planning dialogues have a value in themselves which can influence the control of resource flows, since strategic factors may be taken into account - which means that one or both of the units makes agreements to achieve specific goals.

The above illustrations also point to the problem of separating the internal price rule from organizational processes and contexts.

The Internal Price System as Sediment in the Organization

When this 15-year-old case study was used in January 1991, an interesting discussion developed afterwards with one of the participants. The participant in question worked in the (anonymous) case company, recognised it clearly and was able to provide extensive evidence that the internal pricing system was virtually unchanged from a technical point of view. As a result of other projects, (on calculation principles and in connection with a book on budgeting), I was familiar with the current control system. The question of whether the internal price system has changed from a functional point of view is interesting. The way in which this question is answered depends entirely on how the boundaries for the prices system are defined. If boundaries are defined on the basis of how they affect the internal control of resource flows, at least four changes can be distinguished.

Firstly, from the organization's point of view, major changes occurred when an organizational structure based on business sectors was introduced in the mid-1980's. The intention was to cultivate the opera-tional areas which had strong points of contact with each other. This changed the organization - previously 70 subsidiaries had been directly subordinate to central management. Now, instead, operations were divided up in a manner which correspond to the overall business areas in the organization, thus creating a management structure which was more closely associated with specific fields of operation - something which it may be reasonable to assume ought to have an integrative effect.

Secondly - and more closely linked to the price system - the procedure of crediting subsidiary results backwards in the business sectors has been introduced to supplement a more strict breakdown into profit centers.

Thus, the results of the various units total achievements can be evaluated in relation to the joint effects at the business sector level.

Thirdly, the previous heavily centralized control of marketing units via rates of return has become supplemented to a greater extent by other criteria and measures. This means that although measures such as rates of return are still reported via the central and joint reporting system, it is also possible to place greater emphasis in the various business sectors on specific objectives which are more closely related to the market, for example market share.

Fourthly, the formal calculation system has also been under scrutiny. At one stage, there was particular interest in the company's high capital costs, since there was an awareness that mark-ups based on cost prices might mean limited freedom of action for units which were close to the market. Certain calculation principles have also been modified, for example depreciation.

The fundamental strategy of vertical integration has not changed, subsidiaries in different geographical areas market and service goods in the product areas in which the company operates. That is to say vertical integration continues. However, limiting the question of internal prices to the price system itself does not give an adequate picture. The use of a given system of rules takes place in relation to other parts of the company's control system and organization and can hardly be studied without taking this context into account. This applies particularly when certain aspects of the evaluation of units is tightly coupled to the price system and will thus affect the application and the functioning of the price system. Differing answers may therefore be given to the question of whether the internal price system has changed or not. On the one hand, it may be claimed that the logic of the internal price system and the process for determining price have not changed and that therefore the internal price system remains the same. On the other hand, it may be maintained that even if the fundamental strategy is unchanged, the systems regarding the organization, integration and evaluation of results and the calculation system have changed and that, as a result, the real effects of the internal price system in the organization have changed.

Reflections and conclusions

One important point about negotiating internal prices is that the internal price is no longer unambiguously defined as cost-oriented or market-oriented. Certainly, as in the case study, it is possible to assume either a market-oriented or a cost-oriented model, but in negotiating the intention is that the model is to be confronted by the other assumptions. Correspondingly, a negotiation means that a predetermined model is replaced by a process where the output is not determined in advance. In several respects, therefore, negotiation-based internal prices are a hybrid where neither the model nor the final result are defined unambiguously. It is important to point out in this context that **negotiation refers to the process** and that it is inconsistent to regard negotiation-based prices in the same terms as cost-based and market-based prices. Thus, the process introduces new characteristics to the system which, in themselves, work in different directions.

The situation (and case) described above agrees with the situation defined by Eccles - a vertical strategy with no freedom of action for buying or selling units to decide their sources and their users. Thus, this means that there is considerable interdependence between units, and this makes conflicts highly likely. In addition, in international groups, both buying and selling units must be able to show a profit, for internal as well as for external reasons. The choice of internal pricing model therefore becomes limited. This means, for example, that opportunities for employing models based on marginal cost (as suggested in analogous situations e g by Kaplan and Atkinson) in such situations can scarcely be implemented in practice. The limited opportunity for chosing among models can therefore be compensated by the introduction of negotiations, in particular to give the units concerned a **certain auto-nomy**.

While internal pricing, according to Watson and Baumler, is designed to achieve differentiation because both units become profit oriented, they maintain that negotiation has a partially contrary function: to create **integration**. It should be added that negotiation provides opportunities to take advantage of unique information about the situation of the various units, and thus also to create situational in dependent internal prices. This indicates that one of the purposes of negotiation is also to create **differentiation** on the basis of **different prerequisites**.

In the situation which has been discussed above, only limited guidance is provided by the structurally oriented internal price literature, which focuses, for example, on description of what situational prerequisities are valid for different models. The problem of interdependence between the various units means, amongst other things, that **evaluation** of results will be important both for individual units and in total. This then requires a broader **organizational perspective**, where the use of accounting must also be placed in a social context (cf Bromwich and Bhimani, 1989).

It is particularly important to observe that a process with a **dialogue** between different parties may permit more rapid **problem identification** and **communication** than accounting can normally offer. This also means that studies of the internal price problem should take place to a greater extent under dynamic conditions. This may apply both to protracked historical processes and to crisis circumstances, for example sudden changes in the external environment or organizational upheaval. Such studies might very well supplement analytical or experimental approaches of the type described in the introduction to this paper.

References

Abdel-Khalik, A.R. and Lusk, E.J., (1974), Transfer Pricing - A Synthesis, The Accounting Review, January.

Anthony, R., Dearden, J., Bedford, N., (1989), Management Control Systems, Homewood.

Arwidi, O., (1977), Internationella Koncernen har problem, Lund, (praktikfall).

Arwidi, O., Winqvist, G., (1977), Internprissättning - Perspektivet Komponent i ett Organisationellt System, Lund, EFL.

Arvidsson, G., (1971), Internpriser, Stockholm, EFI.

Bromwich, M. and Bhimani, A., (1989), Management Accounting: Evolution not Revolution,London: The Chartered Institute of Management Accountants.

Chalos, P. and Haka S., (1990), Transfer Pricing under Bilateral Bargaining, The Accounting Review, July.

Cook, P., (1955), Decentralization and the Transfer Price Problem, Journal of Business, April.

Dean, J., (1955), Decentralization and Intracompany Pricing, Harvard Business Review, July-August.

Dearden, J., (1960), Interdivisional Pricing, Harvard Business Review, Vol 38 - No 1.

Eccles, R., (1985), The Transfer Pricing Problem - A Theory for Practice, Lexington.

Frenckner, P., (1954), Internprestationer som Företagsekonomins Bedömningsinstrument, Stockholm.

Hansson, L., (1986), Ekonomistyrning i Divisionaliserade Företag, In Skärvad, P.-H., Controllerhandboken, Stockholm.

Hirschleifer, J., (1956), On the Economics of Transfer Pricing, Journal of Business, July.

Hirschleifer, J., (1957), Economics of the Divisionalized Firm, Journal of Business, April.

Kaplan, R., (1982), Advanced Management Accounting, Englewood Cliffs.

Kaplan, R. and Atkinson, A., (1989), Advanced Management Accounting, Englewood Cliffs.

Shillinglaw, G., (1977), Managerial Cost Accounting, (4:th ed), Homewood.

Solomons, D., (1965), Divisional Performance: Measurement and Control, Homewood.

Tomkins, C., (1990), Making Sense of Cost-Plus Transfer Prices Where There Are Imperfect Intermediate Goods Markets by a " Pragmatic - Analytical " Perspective, Management Accounting Research, Vol 1 no 3.

Vancil, R., (1978), Decentralization: Managerial Ambiquity by Design, Homewood.

Verlage, H., (1975), Transfer Pricing for Multinational Enterprises: Some Remarks on Its Economic, Fiscal and Organizational Aspects, Farnborough.

Watson, D. and Baumler, J., (1975), Transfer Pricing: A Behavioral Context, The Accounting Review, July.

Part 4

Evolution of Corporate Policies

ACTION AND INTENTION
- Closure and Disclosure of Policies

Thomas Polesie
Gothenburg School of Economics
and Commercial Law

Abstract

This essay examines the reciprocal relationship between action and intention in corporate contexts. Closure and disclosure are recurring themes in the inquiry into how information is presented and used.

The study is based on observations of many corporate settings for managerial judgment. The empirical observations have been analyzed with regard to policy issues, communication within the organization and changes in corporate identity.

The basic scheme of analysis regards action and finance as reciprocally related aspects of corporate reality. Mental, physical and financial resources are categories that have been useful in the characterizations of continuity and change over time.

The concluding synthesis sums up some of the experiences from our efforts to understand how the corporate mind works and sometimes does not work.

Introduction

Intention and action are two distinct aspects of what goes on in society. Sometimes they go hand in hand, at other times they belong to different modes of being.

This essay casts some light on the relation between intention and action. In this evasive boarderland we reflect on what is going on around us and deliberate about what to do and what not to do. It is in this process that decisions take shape. They lead on to action, and over the course of time these in turn lead on to reactions from others.

There are many connections between the life of the mind and action (cf Arendt 1978). An elementary 'simplistic' view is to see action as an element of the external world, where its impact is felt in a 'space of appearance'. Another view is to envisage action as a process that goes on inside people. A third view is to take both aspects into account.

"the real action lies not on the surface, in what the characters do ... but within, in their states of mind, ... their theories, and the counterpoint between the thoughts and behaviour of them all, in themselves and in relation to each other ... and in relation to the demands of the indefinable pattern of this world we live in". (Wilkins, preface to Musil 1954, p xvi).

Thoughts come into being and take place - if indeed they do take place - in the recesses of memory and mind. It is our actions that make it possible for others to take part of what we have in mind. Action entails doing something. It has an element of disclosure and communication. Most social acts are carried out with spectators in mind. The people who act may learn to distinguish between front and back regions (cf Goffman, 1959). The front region is designed for disclosure, the back region is closed off. It is not accessible for the spectator. Here, action is rehearsed and the actors can relax without their mask. When all has been said and done, others make their interpretation of the show, respond to it and make their judgment of it.

We will develop a point of view that considers both inner and outer conditions for what goes on. We maintain a distinction between intention, meaning, disclosure and action, but we will also picture some connections between them.

The Conditions for Action and Judgment

Some rules of action say 'look before you leap' - be prudent and careful. Find out what you can about conditions before you do anything. Others say that you might as well go right ahead and do something. In time you will find out what befalls you. This may seem risky, but it is nevertheless a course that most of us sooner or later have to follow.

A reasonable approach to action is to set up some alternatives, to deliberate for a while and then to do something. Some people think a great deal - like Hamlet. They analyze the conditions for action in detail and in doing so they run the risk of losing sight of what is important. They deliberate with themselves for too long and sometimes the time for action never comes. Or, when they finally do make a move, they do the wrong thing and slay Polonius, who was listening in behind a curtain.

Conditions in a corporation sometimes resemble a Shakespearean drama, where anything can happen. Quite often, the organization has been set up so that the people in it don't have much room for deliberation. Under managerial control, the employees are expected to carry out whatever is required of them without gainsay. In 'the domain of everyday action' there is little time for reflection and dialogue (About labour, cf Arendt, 1956).

As the contemporary drama in Eastern Europe has recently reminded us, we all depend on having a day-to-day economy that functions well. We need coffee, soap, cars and electricity. If the supply and demand of these common goods and services functions well, we don't take much notice of them. But, if the flow of goods ceases to function, then we have to do something about it. This may lead to a transformation of a social order (cf Chevardnadzé, 1991).

There is an active side to what goes on, with much 'business', where the invariable objective is to get things done, but there is also a contemplative side - a passive endeavour that seeks understanding, reflection and meaning. A common problem of action is that people's visions and desires don't coincide. Some people want one thing, others want something else.

To envisage something in the mind is a subjective process of imagination. It calls for involvement, commitment and care - 'Sorge' in the language of Heidegger (1969). Our thoughts are not visible to others, nor are they directly accessible. But our thoughts can be disclosed and communicated in a dialogue (cf Levinas 1987). We can let others know what we have in mind - if they care to listen. We can tell them what we wish to do and how we intend to go about it. We can join in a common cause.

The dialogue about intentions, meaning and method is the stuff of corporate policy. In the political process, standpoints are made known. Differences of opinion and conflicts of interest emerge and decisions are taken. As someone's position is disclosed, it becomes an element of the intersubjective discourse in which others take part. As they have their say, they may support or oppose it or bring in other points of view and involve other interests.

To maintain a distinction between closure and disclosure is quite general in policy analyses. As background factors for corporate cohesion and capacity to act, much attention is paid to communicate and maintain the 'belief system' that a company relies on for its smooth functioning (cf Donaldson & Lorsch 1982, Seliger 1976, Clegg 1989)

" ... ideologies are continually adjusted to mask and disguise as customary forms of action that which would otherwise be considered as unreasonable, immoral or illegal." (Tully   p 23).

An observer applies different *perspectives* to phenomena in the life-world. This is illustrated in Allison's classic study of decisions made under the Cuban missile crisis (1971). In an analytical study of this kind, the observer makes his own assumptions about what is relevant (cf Polesie, 1989). His conceptual models determine what he takes note of, and thus what he has to report. These models

"are much more than simple angles of vision or approaches. Each conceptual framework consists of a cluster of assumptions and categories that influence what the analyst finds puzzling, how he formulates his question, where he looks for evidence, and what he produces as an answer. (ibid, p 245).

An external observer assigns importance to phenomena. In most cases he must leave most of what really happened outside his account. Only some aspects of what took place 'on the scene of the crime' are included in the final story, that is disclosed. Many aspects that were present in the closure of the preceding deliberations are surpressed in the final report.

Babel's accounts of the operations of Soviet regiments of horse in Poland are a case in point. He collected his material as a participant in a military expedition in 1920/1. After the fact, he took time for reflection, deliberation and judgment. This process brought new perspectives into the picture.

¨ ... the human fact does not dominate the scene of our existence - for something to 'show forth' it must first be hidden, and the human fact is submerged in and subordinated to a world of circumstance, the world of things; it is known only in glimpses, emerging from the danger or the sordidness in which it is implicated.¨(Trilling in the introduction to Babel's Collected Stories 1974, p 15).

Making Judgments and Taking Action

'Continuity and Change' reports some basic observations of how some organizations in Scandinavia have developed over a five-year period in the 1980:s (cf Polesie 1991) and inquires into how they accumulated experience and competence in their fields of operation. Based on some of these observations we will now develop a line of reasoning about meaning and responsibility for action that was outlined in the synthesis of the study (pp 129-157).

A basic observation is that companies interact with their environment (cf Pfeffer & Salancik 1978). They take in resources from suppliers, transform them into products and services, that they send on to their customers in exchange for revenue. Their ability to survive as independent entities depend on which resources they dispose over and on their ability to maintain a fruitful interaction with others. This interaction is both intersubjective and objective. It requires observations of what the others want and ability to supply it.

A company's competence - its ability to compete - is upheld by a cooperative effort within its organization that puts its resources to use in a meaningful way. At times there are conflicts of interest that disturb this harmonious ideal image.

"An adequate account of human agency must ... be connected to a theory of the acting subject" (Giddens 1979, p 2).

People communicate with each other in many ways. A company's policies - its attitudes and beliefs - can be made known in a dialogue. Habermas (1987) has described how institutional conditions emerge in communicative action.

"In ... understanding-oriented communicative action ... interaction is aimed at achieving an agreement based on a common recognition of validity claims; the presupposition is that this can be done within the context of interaction and without a breakdown in communication." (Mc Carthy 1984, p 290).

The stake-holders in a company reveal their interests in many ways. They try to win respect for them both by argument and by action. Their communicative competence is of different orders.

From time to time, assumptions are re-considered. A constant companion is the need to make out and disclose - to ourselves and others - what we want and why this is so. We try to envisage how results can be brought about. More often than not, we need help from others in the process. We try to strike a balance between what we know we are able to do and what we can accomplish with the help of others and what we actually manage to bring about.

The theme of political judgment has been explored by Arendt (1958, 1968 and 1978) and carried on by Beiner (1983). Spender has also inquired into the nature and sources of judgment in a managerial setting. He has presented some industrial recipes that are grounded in particular contexts and experiences (1989).

Judgments are formed in a process of deliberation that relates subjective elements of experience with objective 'facts'.

"Judgments may be 'analytic' or 'synthetic'. When the premises are complete and consistent, they contain the conclusion. The process of drawing out the conclusion is analytic, strictly logical and closed. ... The process is objective and independent of the deducer who must not add anything to it. 'Synthetic' judgements are open; the conclusion is not contained in the premises alone.
...
In a synthetic decision there must be an active decider. The person judging supplies premises additional to those given in the data, and the conclusion manifests him rather than goes beyond him. He and the conclusion become part of each other. The seeming objectivity of the analytic process disappears. Such creativity brings something of the synthesizers' private self into the social world." (ibid, pp 57)

A comfortable 'anthropological' stance is to be far away from a company under study and to regard it in a neutral way as some kind of 'object'. From this perspective one can make an independent judgment of its product.

"In judging, we enter an implicit claim about the *character* that lies behind such judgments, namely our own." (Beiner 1983, p 136).

Kant viewed judgment as "the faculty of thinking the particular" and to think a particular means to bring it under a general concept (cf Beiner 1982, p 119). An act of judgment subsumes particulars under universal categories. The contingent elements of a concrete setting are thus seen in the light of general concepts. Through this change of perspective, generalized models of the universe and regulative schemes are brought to bear on concrete settings. These various world-views are supported by their respective claims to validity.

Riesman (1952) and Johansson (1989, p 153) have studied people's attitudes with reference to three different tendencies within individuals and societies: tradition-direction, inner-direction and other-direction. These refer to how people perceive reality, how they orient themselves in the world and how they decide what to do.

Some rely on tradition for guidance about what to do. For them, rules and norms are given from experiences and practices in the past. Introverts rely on an inner compass that shows in which direction to go. The needle of their instrument gives direction and thus certainty that comes from within. 'This way is north' or 'we always try to make a profit' as the managers of Vinga would say. Other people are extrovert. They rely on a radar that picks up impulses from the outside world. These signals tell them about what relevant others expect. Riesman developed these categories as follows:

"In the type of society depending upon tradition-direction, social change is at a minimum, though upsets in personal life may be violent and catastrophic.
....

What is central ... to the concept of inner-direction is that one´s life is guided ... by very generalized goals - such as wealth, fame, goodness, achievement ... one never doubts that life is goal-oriented and that the inner voice is the principal source of that direction. ... one may think of such people as gyroscopically driven.
...
the other-directed type whose conformity rests not so much on the incorporation of adult authority as on sensitive attention to the expectations of contemporaries. ... obeys a fluctuating series of short-run goals picked up ... by a radar." (ibid, pp 5).

In her descriptions of the role of Management Information Systems Johansson termed these categories as stabilizer, compass (i e gyroscope) and radar. The interaction between these basic categories can throw light on how a corporate identity may be worked out. Let us explore how 'inner-direction' and 'outer-direction' can be developed as central concepts for describing corporate reality.

Observations of Companies in Action

Printer was a medium-sized company in Denmark (cf Polesie 1991, pp 42 - 45). Its managers set up well-considered policies and made sure that they were accepted in its organization. They worked for a long time to get a consensus about setting up a new department for offset-printing. Their investment in developing computer programmes for type-setting was also an example of a carefully considered policy. The fact that there was a distinct policy helped Printer to overcome the many difficulties with computerizing the process of type-setting. Its managers made a firm commitment to see this project through and they were prepared for a protracted struggle to bring it about. They mobilized the resources that were needed despite the fact that the costs for this venture turned out to be much greater than antecipated. This major investment in type setting subsequently led on to the establishment of a subsidiary in the USA that now has about 100 employees.

Fors made folding rules. It also had a well-established policy for how to develop and modernize its technology for production and marketing. For many years it has maintained a close cooperation with two other producers who made complementary measuring instruments. This alliance gave a basis for joint marketing efforts in Europe and is an embryo for an international group.

Trader and Fors were in much the same commercial position as Printer. Their current operation yeilded a profit and they had an adequate capital base. The group regularly absorbed Fors' profits, but it also supplied means for building a new factory when this was called for.

Profits from the current operation can lead on to self-confidence and this may increase the will to make new investments. It is difficult to abstain from hubris (cf Vinga and Ithaca), even though a better alternative might be to pay taxes and put the remaining money in the bank.

Some of the companies in the study developed favourably, e g Printer, Trader and Fors. Some were in difficulties, e g VIGOR, Arnica and Helios. The ship-yard Ara started its process of change far too late. It did not establish itself on the offshore market in time. It was difficult to succeed in this effort without adequate support from a home market. Beta was taken over by another owner, who had presence on its market and needed its capacity to produce - an integration backwards.

It is easier to act when one has access to adequate resources. VIGOR did not have the resources that were required to continue its business, while Arnica and Ithaca did. Printer also had what was needed for its operation. Trader and Vinga had access to capital and it quickly learned the rules of the game on the market for credit. These companies started up their processes of change in time and therefore managed to stay ahead of their competitors.

The Fur Department regarded its resources and its experience of how to use them as stabilizers under turbulent conditions. Ithaca found a way to cope with rapid change that was based on mutual trust, co-operation and eminent common sense. A similar 'industrial recipe' was found in Arnica and Vinga.

Comprehensive, empirically oriented works give essential material for reflection (cf de Roover 1966, Green & Moss, 1982). They give us access to common points of reference and bases for comparison. Through analysis and critical scrutiny, observations from different settings may be amalgamated into a grounded theory (cf Glaser & Strauss, 1967). An advantage with such a theory is that one knows what it is based are apparent. The lines of argument along which it has emerged. Following this path one can confront and blend experiences from many different sources. As an archive it can help us to make out and interpret what is taking place (cf Foucault, 1972).

Action and Finance - two Aspects of Corporate Reality

We often need to make out relations of many different kinds in order to understand what a company is doing and why. On the one hand, we need to know about the concrete activities that are carried out, on the other hand we need comprehensive measures in money terms.

The flows of activities and money depend on and influence each other reciprocally. A company's identity can manifest itself in the interplay between its financial assets and its activities. There may be many points of transition betweeen these flows and they can be related to each other on many levels.

"Money values do not simply mirror the state of affairs in the real world; valuation is a positive act that makes an impact on the course of events. Monetary and real phenomena are connected in a reflexive fashion; that is, they influence each other mutually. The reflexive relationship manifests itself most clearly in the use and abuse of credit." (Soros 1987, p 17).

To some extent, a company's access to financial means determines which avenues of action that are realistic to set out on (cf Hector, 1988). The language of finance spells out a network of restrictions that influences the commitments that are made. The financial aspect of a company often serves as a simplified measure of value. Measures in money terms can be neutral, but it does happen that they are used as an instrument for enforcing policies - as a language of power and domination (cf Lukes 1974). It is easy to say no in financial terms - 'we cannot afford this'. But, the language of finance can also be used to encourage people and give them openings.

Finance has a built-in tendency to focus single-mindedly on money (cf Hilferding, 1910). At times this is the only total picture we can get.

"If there is one general conclusion which the present study leads to, it is that money - in a manner analogous to the carrier wave - is a means for transmitting signals. It functions as such by means of transactions of conversion on the basis of reciprocity." (Crump 1981, p 291).

Some of the conditions for a company can be expressed in money terms. To spell out a company's financial structure leads to an awareness of how much money that is available. But, the question remains what to do with it.

Resources - mental, physical and financial

Owners sometimes have power in a company. At other times equity capital is just a passive factor on the balance sheet. The owners have made capital available for the company's activities and thus assumed some of the risks of the business. They often make provisions for limiting their personal liability. They set up some of the conditions for the managers and the managers also make some provisions of their own (cf Arendt, 1958 and 'The United States as a seedbed of managerial capitalism', pp 498 in Chandler, 1977).

The relation between total assets and equity can give keys to the relation between a company and its owners. Equity can be built up by accumulating profits in a company - as Trader, Beta, Printer and Fors have done. Fund received its capital 'en bloc' from a pension scheme. It is expected to maintain its market value by making investments in other companies.

Over the years, the managers in Printer have given a great deal of thought to what to do with the revenues from its operation. The company has invested in new printing presses and in design of programmes for text-editing. A separate foundation has been set up to ensure the company's development in the long term.

Equity was a severe restriction in VIGOR, whose owners eventually had to give up. The company had a product that became more and more complicated as customer demands were taken into consideration. If one has sold a product to several large customers, who engage themselves heavily in using it, then pressure for modifications and change are likely to follow. VIGOR would have needed much more resources than it had to meet the requirements for service and re-design that confronted it. But, such resources were not available and the financial restrictions took the upperhand. The company was bought by a competitor, who directed its activities in new directions. After some time, VIGOR's product was replaced by the new owner's product.

Components and Ithaca are two instances of the dialogue between Fund and its partners. When Components needed capital for its activities, it tried to find an owner who was interested in its development and that had sufficient means.

The process in Components illustrates that it is a matter of judgment to work out relations among owners. At first, the investment company A was involved. Then, its place was taken by another investment company B, that had more experience of the industry.

Both Ithaca and Components rely heavily on know-how for their development. They have made determined efforts to grow. Without the financial backing of Fund they would not have been able to forge ahead the way they have done.

With the financial backing of Fund, Components could launch its project on the European scene, where it worked with partners and customers that were much larger than itself. The company knew what it wanted to do and needed more resources than it could raise on its own. As things have turned out, Fund has contributed to its development without dictating its business policy.

Fund had a portfolio of marketable shares, from which it could withdraw at will. Investments in non-public companies were not so easy to quit (about the 'exit-option', cf Hirschman, 1970). There was no established market for these shares. These investments rely on trust and mutual respect and call for a greater presence in the operation of the company.

Fund established a network of contacts to work through. It has created stable conditions that made it possible for companies to take initiatives and develop. Fund has extended the capital base for Components and Ithaca.

The study has examined 6 state-owned agencies that have been set up under public control. One may well wonder if their business judgments are made on grounds that are any different from privately owned companies.

Ara and Beta show that companies will act under pressure, regardless of who owns them. An essential question of identity is whose company they are. Who is their master? Where are their loyalties? Do they believe that their policy is right? For how long can they keep on struggling? (cf Hayes, 1987, Arendt, 1978, Green & Moss, 1982). By which means do they 'legitimate' their actions unto themselves and others? Invariably it takes imagination, patience and perseverence to develop the relations between principal, agent and action in a fruitful way.

The issue of ownership is fundamental for delimiting a corporate entity and working out the conditions for its supply of capital. These considerations concern who will assume responsibility for activities and take the consequences of what happens - for better or worse.

Reading the Corporate Mind

Companies stand for action in the community. Their space of appearance is the 'vita activa' (Arendt 1958, pp 175). Businessmen and managers are constantly 'doing business'. They make things and they make deals with each other. At times they also try to influence the course of society at large.

The passive side shows who the financial stake-holders of a company are. Equity is a catch-all concept that ensures the closure of the accounting model. Equity indicates that some owners has made capital available for the company to work with. This gives its managers discretion to act. It also holds them responsible for what they do and what they let be.

Closure is an element of managerial control. In this arena managers are expected to have full information about what goes on in the organization. Financial accounting is what they disclose to outsiders - which is often far from all they actually know about the company. Openness is an essential requisite for internal communication in an organization. Closure is needed to focus and condense the reports that are disclosed to the outside world.

The development-process in Vinga resembles what happened in Arnica. Both companies were governed from the centre, though they employed many action-oriented people who took care of the daily activities of the organization. They had efficient information systems that facilitated local action.

Arnica suspended its payments, while Vinga was able to make ends meet. It spread its risks, though its offshore-venture brought the company close to the edge of a break-down. The stable parts in the group - the stabilizers - gave support to those parts that were exposed to risks. Arnica did not give up after the financial collapse. The company managed to raise fresh capital and continued its activities. Its capital base had been moved abroad, but its operation was much the same as before.

Business relations are inherently conservative and cumulative. Once a company has found a niche, it has strong tendencies to stick to it. It often makes great efforts to work its way into such a position and once it is there it regards this corner of the world as its own, e g Salt, Fors and Vinga Line.

Vinga is a formidable actor on its markets - competent and competitive. Through a series of mergers and acquisitions it now controls the largest system of ferry-services in the world. One could say that Vinga has an 'inner-directed' drive - its compass says that the company must make money at all times. In order to reach this objective it uses brokers, radar, stunt-fliers, auto-pilots and many other agents for scanning its markets (cf Johansson 1989 about 'stunt-fliers' and 'auto-pilots').

Printer developed its resources over long timecycles. Other companies, like Goldsmith, acted first and were forced to think about the consequences afterwards. The situation on the maritime market forced the managers of West-bay into a retreat. In other cases, e g Steel-mill, ideas about cooperation with a European partner were a long time brewing before the external conditions became right for transforming them into action.

The transition from intention to action has bearing on the development of corporate identity. At times, action grows organically by way of an internal dialogue, as in Micro. In other instances it is the outcome of a struggle for power as in Steel-mill, or through a change of owner as in Beta and VIGOR.

The domain of action - what we actually do - can be extended by learning new things. In Ithaca, one has always known a great deal about how to run ships, but in the course of the study one also learned about how the world of finance works and how it does not work (cf Soros, 1987). Ithaca was a platform from which people acted in concert. Its employees knew that they are expert seamen and this gave them a stable identity. They sold transport services to others and used the revenues to develop their company. Ithaca has grown steadily, and so has Vinga. But, for how long can these shipping companies keep on growing (cf Green & Moss, 1982)?

Donaldson & Lorsch presented some conclusions about how managers' 'beliefs' become visible as a company changes:

"... the reshaping of corporate direction involves reshaping the underlying belief systems.
...
Basic changes in corporate strategy do happen; but they require a long lead-time ... and above all, a shared personal conviction that the survival of the firm is the critical goal.
...
If ... managers believe that corporate survival is at stake, they will extricate their strategy from their beliefs and make appropriate changes - however painful the process." (1983, p 158)

A company's policy outlines what it wants to accomplish and which means it intends to use along the way. The images of what do acquire validity in small steps as they are absorbed by the people in the organization (cf Morgan, 1986). They are confirmed by activities in practice. The process of making conditions clear may go on for a long time. Many reactions need to be taken into consideration in the process.

It may be a straightforward undertaking to describe conditions and activities in companies that develop their policies in an open dialogue such as Ithaca, Fors and Arnica, where investments were of common interest. It is quite natural to discuss policies in open-minded companies like Micro, Vinga and Components. It is more difficult to describe the use of resources in tightly controlled companies like Trader, Printer and Ara, where information was not circulated outside the small circle of people who took the decisions.

It takes courage to speak up when a company's strategy is not working as it should be. The managers in Ara were squeezed in between the demands from the group and the economic facts of the operation. The managers in Helios and Steel-mill also found it difficult to maintain their policies in the face of disapproval from the central managers.

A recurring theme in the study has been to establish trust and the will to assume responsibility (cf Jonas, 1984, Olson, 1982). Havel has also taken up this theme as an essential aspect of identity.

"the notion of human responsibility ... has begun to appear ... as that fundamental point from which all identity grows and by which it stands or falls

...

identity provides ... a vantage point from which the various questions of human existence may be mapped out ... " (Havel 1990, p 145.)

The people who present and re-present a company do things, and assume responsibility for what they do.

"human responsibility ... assumes the existence of two poles: a person who is responsible, and someone, or something, for whom or for which he is responsible." (Havel 1990, p 145.)

Our interpretations of what we have observed give points of departure for analyses and syntheses. We have highlighted some corporate contexts and found similarities and differences between them. The theories we have found in use are the 'givens' of managerial beliefs.

Impulses can come from the outside, but perception, beliefs, experience and action come from the inside.

Someone who assumes responsibility for something, gives it meaning and does what he can to see it through. But, only someone with an identity of his own can be absorbed completely by his activities and thus put all of his resources into the struggle for some common cause.

References

Allison, G. T., (1971), Essence of Decision. Explaining the Cuban Missile Crisis, Boston: Little, Brown & Co.

Arendt, H., (1958), The Human Condition, Chicago: University of Chicago Press.

Arendt, H., (1968), Between Past and Future: Eight Exercises in Political Thought. Enlarged edn, New York: Viking Press.

Arendt, H., (1978), The Life of the Mind, (Vol. 1 Thinking, Vol. 2 Willing), New York: Harcourt Brace & Jovanovich.

Babel, I., (1974), Collected Stories, Penguin Modern Classics: Harmondsworth.

Beiner, R., (1982), Hannah Arendt on Judging. Interpretive Essay, Part Two of Arendt.

Beiner, R., (1983), Political Judgment, Chicago: Univ. of Chicago Press.

Chevardnadzé, E., (1991), L'avenir s'écrit liberté, Ed Odile Jacob, Paris.

Clegg, S. R., (1989), Frameworks of Power, London: Sage.

Crump, T., (1981), The Phenomenon of Money, London: Routledge & Kegan Paul.

Donaldson, G. and Lorsch, J. W., (1983), Decision Making at the Top. The Shaping of Strategic Direction, New York: Basic Books.

Foucault, M., (1972), The Archaeology of Knowledge, London: Tavistock.

Giddens, A., (1979), Central Problems in Social Theory. Action, Structure and Contradiction in Social Analysis, London: Macmillan.

Giddens, A., (1984), The Constitution of Society. Outline of the Theory of Structuration, Cambridge: Polity Press.

Giddens, A., (1991), Modernity and Self-Identity. Self and Society in the Late Modern Age, Stanford California: Stanford Univ. Press.

Glaser, B. G. and Strauss, A. L., (1967), The Discovery of Grounded Theory: Strategies for Qualitative Research, New York: Aldine de Gruyter.

Green, E. and Moss, M. A., (1982), Business of National Importance. The Royal Mail Shipping Group, 1902-1937, London: Methuen.

Goffman, E., (1990), The Presentation of Self in Everyday Life, Anchor Books (1959), Reprint, London: Penguin Books.

Habermas, J., (1979), Communication and the Evolution of Society, Boston: Beacon Press.

Habermas, J., (1987), The Theory of Communicative Action, Vol 1 and 2, Cambridge: Polity Press.

Havel, V., (1990), Letters to Olga, London: Faber & Faber.

Hayes, P., (1987), Industry and Ideology. I G Farben in the Nazi Era, Cambridge: Cambridge Univ. Press.

Hector, G., (1988), Breaking The Bank, Boston: Little, Brown & Co.

Hilferding, R., (1981), Finance Capital. A study of the latest phase of capitalist development, (1910), London: Routledge & Kegan Paul.

Hirschman, A ., (1970), Exit, Voice and Loyalty. Responses to Decline in Firms, Organizations and States, Cambridge, Mass.: Harvard Univ. Press.

Johansson, I-L., (1989), Människor och ekonomi - en studie av hur säljare använder ekonomisystem i tre framgångsrika företag, Göteborg: BAS.

Jonas, H., (1984), The Imperative of Responsibility, Chicago: Univ. of Chicago Press.

Jönsson, S., (1990), Action Research, Paper for the ISRA-90 Workshop in Copenhagen.

Kant, I., (1952), The Critique of Judgement, Oxford: Clarendon Press, First edition 1790.

Kilmann, R.H. and Covin, T. J, (1988), Corporate Transformation. Revitalizing Organizations for a Competitive World, S. Francisco: Jossey Bass Publ.

Levinas, E., (1987), Time and the Other, Pittsburgh, Pennsylvania: Duquesne Univ. Press.

Lukes, S., (1974), Power. A radical view, London: Macmillan, (reprinted 1990).

McCarthy, T., (1978), The Critical Theory of Jürgen Habermas, Cambridge: Polity Press.

Morgan, G., (1986), Images of Organization, Beverly Hills: Sage.

Morgan, G., (1988), Riding the Waves of Change, S. Francisco: Jossey Bass Publ.

Musil, R., (1954), The Man without Qualities, Vol 1-3, London: Picador.

Olson, O., (1982), Ansvar och ändamål, Lund: Doxa.

Pfeffer, J. and Salancik, G., (1978), The External Control of Organizations. A Resource Dependence Perspective, New York: Harper & Row.

Polesie, T., (1981), Action and Reaction - Decisive Factors in Developing Accounting Systems, Accounting, Organizations and Society, Vol 6, No 2, pp 167-174.

Polesie, T., (1988), Certainty and Uncertainty - Two Basic Factors in the Design and Use of an Accounting System, In: Bedriftsökonomiens helhet. Spenning mellom analyse og humaniora, Eds. Holmesland T and Ims K J, Bergen: Alma Mater.

Polesie, T., (1989), An Inquiry into the Relevance of Information in three Swedish Companies, In: Etudes en Compabilité International, Eds. D Boussard & P Delvaille, Ecole Superieure de Commerce de Paris.

Polesie, T., (1991), Continuity and Change - Corporate Identity in a Scandinavian Perspective, Göteborg: BAS.

Riesman, D., (1951), The Lonely Crowd: A Study of the Changing American Character, New Haven: Yale Univ. Press.

Riesman, D., (1965), Faces in the Crowd, New Haven: Yale Univ. Press, Abridged edition.

de Roover, (1966), The Rise and Decline of the Medici Bank 1397-1494, New York: Norton.

Seliger, M., (1976), Ideology and Politics, London: George Allen & Unwin.

Skinner, Q., (1978), The Foundations of Modern Political Thought, Cambridge: Cambridge Univ. Press.

Soros, G., (1987), The Alchemy of Finance. Reading the Mind of the Market, New York: Simon & Schuster.

Spender, J - C., (1989), Industry Recipes. The Nature and Sources of Managerial Judgement, London: Basil Blackwell.

Tully, J., ed. (1988), Meaning and Context. Quentin Skinner and his Critics, London: Polity Press.

ENTREPRENEURSHIP - THE MANAGEMENT OF AMBIGUITY

Bengt Johannisson
Växjö University and Lund University

Abstract

Entrepreneurs operate on the market as both anarchists and organizers. They question the current order as a means to create a new order in terms of e g a new product or production/distribution technology. While other actors on the market strive for uncertainty reduction and practice cost management, entrepreneurs seek opportunities and manage ambiguity. Ultimately the destruction/construction processes designed by the entrepreneur imply manipulation of institutionalized constructions of reality. Physical artifacts such as products and material resources only partially reflect the taken-for-granted order put in question by the entrepreneur. Generically speaking, entrepreneurs thus challenge existing patterns of meaning and establish their own.

To realize new images of reality implies enacting alien environments. This calls for experiental learning where small gains and losses hopefully combine and give success. In order to be able to adopt this experiential learning strategy as well as impose it on others, the entrepreneur must have self-confidence.

Self-confidence is then refueled through rationalization of actions taken, whether successful or not. This rationalization process calls for versatile tools, including e g equivocal verbal actions and an illusive organization, the personal network. Entrepreneurs fulfill their function as ambiguity managers in the marketplace by adopting similar vehicles for the management of their own venturing process.

Postmodern Time Management

In this so-called "postmodern" age, conventional wisdom is obsolete and replaced with notions such as "anything goes" in "a fragmented society". Organizing principles associated with linear time and physical space are abandoned in a context where communication technology provides unlimited combinations of what is supposed to be images of "reality". While this emerging chaos alienates most people, intellectuals thrive. Entrepreneurs too. Turbulence thus provides both uneasiness and opportunity. This applies to society in general as well as to the business community in particular.

While management research is mainly concerned with finding ways to avoid environmental uncertainty, studies of entrepreneurship should be concerned with the recognition of the opportunities which the new age brings forth. Up until the 1970s entrepreneurs were basically looked upon as promoters of innovations which creatively disrupted the existing order in the marketplace. In the postmodern era their mission seems to be as much a question of bringing order to chaotic realities. The entrepreneur deals with the social reality in the manner in which anybody, with the help of a kaleidoscope, can mechanically create order (over and over again) of a chaotic "reality" of pieces of coloured glass. In the latter case time is synchronized sequentially; entrepreneurs have to cope with synchronicity holistically, have to practice "timing management".

The field of entrepreneurial studies is however confused, to a great extent due to varying paradigmatic (and thus usually implicit) assumptions. Most studies and textbooks are based upon an "objectivist" approach (Burrell & Morgan, 1979), i e consider the entrepreneur to be an economic actor with the function to introduce, more efficiently, ways in which to use available physical and financial resources for existing or new ends. The entrepreneurs are expected to belong to a very rare species with unique talents. The question about how this capability is achieved and used to take advantage of market opportunities is nevertheless dealt with in a paradoxical way. On the one hand it is suggested that entrepreneurs have qualitative abilities that are beyond systematic inquiry, such as vision and intuition; on the other hand opportunity-management courses are offered at several academic and other institutions.

In my opinion current research reduces entrepreneurship to a concern for the early stages of what is considered to become a growing venture. The association of entrepreneurship with small-scale family business is in the literature considered to be a regrettable restriction which the introduction of adequate functional management should make up for. This explains the overwhelming interest in the 1980:s for corporate entrepreneurship and the creation of entrepreneurial cultures within corporate settings. These cultures aim at re-enforcing appropriate personal attributes. However, there are many other options available to research into entrepreneurship, besides that of yielding to psychological reductionism. The concept of entrepreneurship could e g be widened and embrace studies of (evolving) entrepreneurial careers. More important, though, is that definitions must relate to contemporary society where fragmentation even pertains to the large corporations as well. Today the entrepreneur's role as a "creative constructor" seems to be as crucial as her/his traditional Schumpetarian role as a "creative destructor."

Before a new concept of entrepreneurship can be provided, a review of paradigmatic assumptions is needed (Section 2). The inquiries into entrepreneurs as managers of ambiguity calls for further discussion of the notion of reality as a social construction and the implications of this notion for entrepreneurship (Section 3). In Section 4 unique features of entrepreneurial networks as the entrepreneur's major tool in her/his reality-creating and organizing processes are discussed. An outline of an action theory of entrepreneurship and ambiguity management is presented in Section 5. The final section summarizes the arguments in the perspective of conventional wisdom.

Alternative Paradigms and Entrepreneurship Research

Most entrepreneurial research that denies an objectivist approach is reduced to "abstracted empiricism", i e applies a subjectivist approach

157

to ontology, epistomology and assumptions about human nature and then shortly degenerates into methodology associated with the objectivist approach in the empirical confrontation (Burell & Morgan 1979:104-106). While the need for visionary thinking and acting is recognized, case reports and qualitative research are at the same time considered to be "anecdotal" information. Obviously most students of entrepreneurship are snared in their opinion that reality is externally given to the individual.

Along with proponents of the objectivist approach I share the notion of the entrepreneur as the person who designs the process that ultimately creates new patterns of business transactions. In basically all other respects I have a divergent view, including the way these new flows of transactions are created. By decoupling the notion of entrepreneurship from the assumption of an objectively existing reality, the confusing linkages to normative management models can also be severed. If reality is considered to be the socially negotiated product of human consciousness and known only through experience, then entrepreneurship is more related to creative action in general than with management of physical, financial and human capital (employees' formal knowledge). Entrepreneurs also use intuition, tacit knowledge, social capital and personal networks in their construction of reality (Johannisson 1990).

Within functionalist organization theory the main objective of formal organizations is seen to be uncertainty reduction, cf e g Thompson 1967. Contingency models of organizations often include environmental uncertainty as a major parameter. The assumption is that uncertainty is a finite property that interferes with the effective management of economic activity. Recent developments within economics and organization theory, e g the transaction-cost approach (Williamsson, 1979), also see uncertainty in exchange relationships as something that has to be reduced. While Williamson suggests internalization, followers within the field of industrial organization and marketing argue that stable supplier/customer networks often offer a more adequate response, cf e g Håkansson, 1982. However, these approaches are all biased towards structure, stability and harmony. In my opinion the full potential of the network as a frame for organizing processes is then not fully exploited and furthermore the use of ambiguity and tension for both pro-action and re-action is depreciated.

Recognition of the dynamics of "ambiguity" depends then very much on the applied paradigm and associated definition of the concept. According to The American Heritage Dictionary (2nd Ed) ambiguity refers to both "susceptible of multiple interpretation" and "doubtful or uncertain". According to The Concise Oxford Dictionary ambiguity means both "of double meaning" and "obscure". While the first group of definitions are positively loaded, or at least neutral, the second are derogatory. In political life and diplomacy the use of ambiguous statements is recognized as an indispensible means to deal with unexpected and emerging realities while at the same time saving one's own and the counterpart's face.

March and Olsen (1976:12) relate ambiguity in organizations basically to a situation where insufficient information concerning cause-and-effect relationships prevail. However, they also argue that organizational goals and attention are often ambiguouos. Weick (1979:180) defines the associated concept "equivocality" as a communication situation where the recipient cannot decide which one of alternative inputs that produce the output message. Meyerson and Martin (1986:174) distinguish between "uncertainty" ("...external or environmental sources of unpredictable change...") and "ambiguity" ("...internal mental confusion caused by complextity and lack of clarity...". These definitions reveal their belief in an "objective" world. Whether this is the case or the environment is considered to be "enacted" (Weick, 1979), experiential learning seems to be the proper way to deal with it. Within corporate strategy research Kylén (1989) has shown that cognitive models with their bias for simplicity and action can, much better than analytical or cybernetic models, explain how business corporations deal with uncertainty which is due to radical environmental change.

Adopting a subjectivist approach, ambiguity refers to the fact that individuals, including diplomats and entrepreneurs, perceive the environment differently, with reference to what they see, how they process their perceptions and to what extent they take action based on

159

earlier experience. Neither politicians nor businessmen have to be visionary in order to "see" what they believe.

While most people are attracted by collectively defined and harmonized perceptions, entrepreneurs pursue divergent perceptions with conviction. In contrast to fanatics they simultaneously uphold their ability to learn and realize which parts of the environment are too "objectified" to be changed, cf Berger & Luckmann (1966). They are capable both of re-acting and pro-acting and of inter-acting, cf below. The entrepreneurs' active participation in the making of their own reality is encompassed in every-day maxims: entrepreneurs are supposed to take action, take initiative, take responsibility. Nobody gives them assignments, tells them what to do.

Subjectivist approaches within the social sciences ascribe any human being capabilites of enacting their own environments in spite of the fact that radical organization theorists argue that dominating structures, primarily capitalism, alienate most persons. My own research suggests that the optimistic and pessimistic interpretation of human discretion in contemporary society can be reconciled if the sociobiological development of individuals is taken into account. In childhood most people mobilize creativity and enact it in play (Johannisson 1989, March 1976); most adults self-impose a straitjacket of restrictions. Paradox and ambiguity are actively dealt with only in humour and poetry, cf Koestler 1964. Some individuals remain naive and continue to play, now with society - if the play-ground is the market I call these "entrepreneurs". In contrast to orthodox advocates of the subjectivist outlook I thus argue that for various reasons only some people, including the entrepreneurs, appear to be the fully conscious, autonomous and free-will actors that the paradigm postulates. I may therefore be accused of trying to combine consensus- and conflict-oriented paradigms in the Burrell/Morgan scheme. My defense is that to me its subjectivist/objectivist distinction seems to be the more decisive one in scientific inquiry. Nevertheless the notion of "management" should not be reserved for approaches within an objectivist paradigm, but apply generally to the systematic use of a mode of organizing resources - or meaning, cf e g Smircich & Morgan, 1982.

Entrepreneurship in a Socially Constructed World

If "reality" is considered to be interpretations of perceptions, structures, whether they concern societal norms or formal organizations, appear as negotiated orders which, once recognized, are reinforced by human interaction, cf Berger & Luckmann, 1966. Most people adopt different roles as they take part in various negotiated orders: the family, the neighbourhood, the workplace, the professional association. By adopting ascribed roles, energy is saved that is needed to balance divergent role commitments. My argument is that such commitments seem to increase in postmodern society.

Interpretive sociologists consider reality to be evolving and any formal structure to be provisional. This suggests that individual actions and "trans-actions" should be seen as the ultimate building block in organizing processes. Ideally regularity in the exchange generates symmetric relationships. However, since most individuals take certain aspects of their reality for granted, some relationships turn out to be asymmetric. Paternalism rules in most families and family businesses while managers are superiors at work. Since people are born into a social context furnished with institutions, i e "taken-for-granted" patterns of relationships, the discretionary sphere becomes considerably reduced.

Entrepreneurs oppose externally imposed orders in as much as the latter restrict their latitude to realize their own visions. Entrepreneurs prefer to have transactions structured in a way that reflects and enforces their own personality and venture. Freedom of action can be achieved by exit or initiative. Exit means that the present action frame is deserted for one which is more in line with the individual's outlook. The alternative is to change the existing order in the context where the entrepreneur operates. Usually this means increasing ambiguity in terms of introducing new realities, whether in terms of a new product or in terms of a new way of interpreting changing market values. If a new order is to become enacted the old one has first to be unlearned. As indicated above, entrepreneurs, like leaders, also have a unique capability for creating order in chaotic situations, i e ability to reduce externally imposed ambiguity, cf Smircich & Morgan, 1982, Czarniawska-Joerges & Wolff, 1989.

The entrepreneur's venturing process, whether initially a destruction or construction process, will not necessarily be successful. The outcome is dependent upon the stretchability of existing objectified structures and counteracting forces mobilized by parties who want to defend or introduce their ways of interpreting the situation. Two mechanisms, however, increase the odds for the entrepreneur. Firstly, (s)he does not create a new world view her/himself but rather identifies and enforces favorable changes spontaneously initiated into the environment. They are able to surf on external events and alertly synchronize these with own actions, cf Drucker, 1985. Their supposed pro-active profile is thus partially illusionary. Secondly, motivation and willingness to work long hours enables the entrepreneur to make up for mistakes along the road. Reality is constantly rearranged by rationalizations of previous actions and new actions. Perseverance and incremental changes will make a more efficient learning process and reinforce self-reliance, cf Weick, 1984.

As indicated above, the adopted paradigm also defines the means available to carry out the entrepreneurial endeavour. Within an objectivist approach physical and financial assets are held up since they are always scarce in ventures with liabilities of newness and uniqueness. Within a subjectivist paradigm on the contrary, human and social resources are in focus. Formal competences may very well be recognized as resources within the objectivist approach but within a subjectivist approach competences such as resourcefulness, reflected experience, intuitive insight are not only taken into account but highlighted (Reuber et al 1990). The entrepreneur has the capability and self-confidence to make use of unique human resources.

Within a subjectivist approach cognitive learning theories, as provided by e g Kolb et al, 1984 and Argyris & Schein, 1978, must be supplemented with emotional aspects, including commitment and willpower. An interesting approach of nature kind is provided by Brunsson (1985), who is nevertheless biased towards the manner in which large organizations take action in spite of restrictions imposed through formal decision structures. Lessem's (1984) application of the notion of "Action Learning" to entrepreneurship does however pay due respect to emotional factors.

Decision and action both imply choice. In formal structures such choices are presented as analytical or negotiating procedures. In the entre–preneurial world, choices are closer to a laying of a puzzle. However, in the entrepreneurial world the whole picture precedes the pieces of the puzzle. The entrepreneur starts off with a holistic vision, her/his image of the completed puzzle. To materialize that vision the entrepreneur must be able to identify ingredients in the imaged reality in a way that makes it possible to fit already existing pieces into the envisioned picture. In order to succeed, the entrepreneur must then be able to rationalize choices and placement both for her/himself and for environmental actors. (S)he must also believe in serendipity, i e that coincidence may supply pieces to complete the puzzle - believing is seeing, (cf above and Weick, 1976, 1979).

The "Garbage-Can" model of organizational choice provided by Cohen, March, Olsen and others, cf e g March & Olsen, 1976, appears to be a feasible approach to entrepreneurial choice. It could even be argued that its application to entrepreneurial realities may justify the model. Once developed to enhance the understanding of institutionalized pathologies in educational systems, the model has been criticized for not bringing any substantial conclusions for organizational design. In my mind the model "makes sense" when applied to the field of entrepreneurship.

The contribution of the "Garbage-Can" model to a theory of (entre-preneurial) action is however limited. The originators of the Garbage-Can model try to explain ongoing processes with organization members' limited rationality and information processing capacity. They include "liking" as a determinant of choice but emotions are not explicitly dealt with. Individuals are basically seen as reacting to environmental change. A fully-fledged subjectivist approach would create a better understanding of how strong-willed individuals, such as politically talented managers, cf Quinn, 1978, Normann, 1977, as well as entrepreneurs, can use organizing settings for rationalizing in their own interest. However, several contributions from the Garbage-Can model to an action theory of entrepreneurship remain.

Firstly, "garbage" and chaos mean economizing with the energy needed for unlearning before the entrepreneur can impose an own structure, implicitely designed by her/his mental map. Therefore entrepreneurial organizations, which often appear to others as chaotic, provide the entrepreneur with a self-evident structure. The "Garbage-Can" model recognizes ambiguities with respect to e g goals, history, technology and the definition of organization boundaries. Since the creative venturing process per se is the entrepreneur's prime mover and her/his personal history is disguised to others, (s)he can ensure any goal's feasiblility, if need be. Along the same line cause/ means pattern of history and technology can be continuously reconstructed by an entrepreneur who is carried by a vision (Mintzberg, 1973, Normann, 1977). Below I will elaborate on why the entrepreneur organizes her/his venture both strategically and spontaneously by way of networking across firm boundaries.

Secondly, in the "Garbage-Can" model, choices are seen as spontaneous coordination of quite independent and largely uncontrollable "streams" of actors, problems, solutions and gatherings where choices can be made, i e actors who bear a problem or a solution can compare, adjust and combine. While strategic management recommends more structure to reduce the uncertainty created, entrepreneurs try to enforce ambiguity since in such a context their unique competences in terms of "seeing" and "realizing" new opportunities come to the fore. By reframing they turn, on the one hand, problems into solutions (to problems posed by other people) and, on the other hand, taken-for-granted solutions into problems (in order to be able to present own alternative solutions). Entrepreneurs who listen to critical customers and turn their complaints into product-development initiatives illustrate the first case (Peters, 1988). The latter situation reflects the classical function of the entrepreneur, that of "the creative destruction" (Schumpeter, 1934).

The original "Garbage-Can" model also states what measures taken by the actor are important in order to understand why, how and what

164

decisions are made. March & Olsen (1976) mainly resorts passive factors such as spending time on being present in the organization and investing energy on attention. While entrepreneurs also recognize these factors, they do not restrict strategic action to existing access and influence structures but create and maintain personal access routes on own initiative. Thereby they more successfully can impose their own images of reality.

The metaphor of the organization as a garbage-can relates to the notion of organizations as a "loosely coupled system", a metaphor also applied to educational organizations (cf Weick, 1976). The notion of loose coupling includes e g situations where several means produce the same end, absence of regulation and prerequisites, poor observational capabilities on the part of a viewer and lack of coterminus of an organization's structure and its activity (1976:5). Several advantages are associated with loose coupling, including e g provision of a qualified sensing mechanism, sealing off of breakdowns and preservation of the identity of elements.

Further inquiries into the notion of loose coupling and entrepreneurship calls for a comment on the notion of "organization". Firstly, within a social-construction perspective "organizing" is a more appropriate concept than "organization". The enacted reality is constantly remoulded. Secondly, the material representation of the frame within which these reality-constructing processes are going on is not the entrepreneurial firm but the firm and its "context" (Johannisson 1988). Contexts include both spatially demarcated, e g the local community or the science park, and functionally demarcated, e g the corporation, action frames. By way of "economies of overview" the entrepreneur operates her/his own firm tightly and exploits the advantages of loose coupling within the context (Johannisson 1990a).

The entrepreneur's ability to operate on both firm and context level means that (s)he can overcome some of the disadvantages of (contexts as) loosely coupled systems. The context is not selective in reinforcing success patterns; the entrepreneur is. The context provides weak responses to environmental changes; the entrepreneur may react strongly to weak signals. While management of change is difficult on the contextual level, the entrepreneurial firm is the vehicle for change in the market, cf Weick , 1976, pp 6-9.

A crucial factor for the understanding of the entrepreneur as a social constructor and manager of ambiguity is her/his intrinsic motivation and reward. The creation, the "making", of the business venture is the meaning of entrepreneurial life. It is the "making" of new business that makes entrepreneurs tick. The concept of "flow", introduced by Csikszentmihalyi (1985) connotates the extended peak experiences that drive committed people. To suggest that material rewards "cause" these people to complete their missions is obviously misdirected. Nevertheless most "management knowhow" developed in the field and public programmes to support new venture creation are based on this misconception.

Organizing New Realities - Entrepreneurial Networking

Human interaction stands out as crucial for recognizing reality as a social construction (Weick 1979). Even the individual as an ego is defined by his/her social relationships, by the personal network. Communication builds and socializes individually created images. Within radical approaches, represented by e g Jurgen Habermas, symmetric communication and exchange is fundamental for the development of any reality, i e the world in general. The personalized character of network exchange then is pivotal. Berger and Luckmann (1966) state that face-to-face contacts are superior as a tool in the construction of reality. Written communication excludes instant dialogue and emotional charge, telephone calls exclude the body language.

My own empirical research states that entrepreneurs engage in symmetric, personalized networking (Johannisson 1983, 1987, 1990, Johannisson & Spilling, 1986). By organizing his/her business activities in this way the entrepreneur can integrate the career on the market with every-day life. Energy is released which can be used to challenge taken-for-granted mental and physical structures in the marketplace. It is not surprising that empirical research shows that social ties are as important as business ties in emerging entrepreneurial networks (Johannisson, 1990). This finding is not only due to blunt survey methodology. Within a subjectivist approach entrepreneurs are expected to have difficulties in separating commercial and social concerns.

Personal networks are potent because they include all kinds of commitment and rationality - instrumental, affective and moral (Kanter, 1972, Sjöstrand, 1986). The network as it emerges provides an extended organization that is on the one hand tailored to the entrepreneur's personality, on the other hand links his/her egocentric network into the context (Johannisson 1987). The network provides a socioeconomic tissue ready for alternative uses (cf Bougon & Steyfert, 1990, Brytting, 1991). On the one hand the network has a considerable capacity for absorbing both internally and externally generated changes, on the other hand it is difficult "manage", cf Weick, 1976. While a formal organization is perceived as an established but alien structure by the entrepreneur, the network is both selfevident and elusive.

The personal network "makes sense" to the entrepreneur as (s)he enacts the environment and provides perceived overview (Johannisson, 1990a) that builds selfconfidence and promotes action. Concretely the sense-making process e g means that the entrepreneur uses his/her network to extend the storage capacity for alternative images and experiences. The network also retains resources from realized, but abandoned, ventures as well as ideas concerning conceived but never launched ventures. These resources carried by the network are submitted to reciprocal general commitments and access is based on tacit knowledge. The formal structure of entrepreneurial venturing, the "firm", then appears as an externally imposed construct, artificially "bracketing" part of the emerging personal network and venture. The basic processual character of the entrepreneurial endeavour is not changed.

The argument, which is illustrated in Figure 1 below, has three major implications. Firstly, realized ventures only reflect part of entre-preneurs' venturing process. Secondly, recycling of resources carried by the network is crucial for entrepreneurs. Thirdly, what to outsiders may appear as a quite unrelated sequence of individual ventures reflects to the entrepreneur her/himself a consistent and self-evident logic.

A common subject for discussion within entrepreneurial research is which unit of analysis to adopt. Suggestions include the entrepreneur as a person (Carland et al, 1988) and the individual venture as the outcome of an apersonal process (Gartner, 1989). Cf also Chell, 1985. If reality is considered to be successively moulded out of interpersonal action, the entrepreneur and her/his set of ventures as they develop together over time into a career should be the unit of analysis. It materializes in temporally and spatially interconnected ventures. At any given point in time a specific venture/project represents the focus for entrepreneurial action but the entrepreneur's personal network allows the various experiences sediment and integrate. This integration concerns both various ventures within the business operations and reconciliation of the entrepreneur's business side with her/his behavior and action in other life spheres.

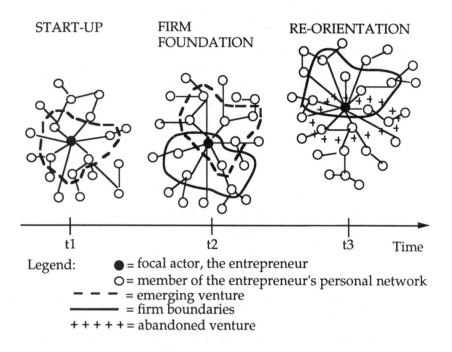

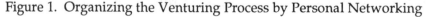

Figure 1. Organizing the Venturing Process by Personal Networking

Spontaneous networking promotes serendipetous venture initiation. Once launched, the venture will need supplementary resources which a resourceful network can provide. The "general reciprocity" that personalized ties imply means that imbalances in one relationship/venture can be reduced by providing other services/engagements in other ventures. The personal network takes on different roles over the different phases of individual ventures (Johannisson, 1990) and entrepreneurial careers (Johannisson, 1987). Thus, the entrepreneurial career can only be fully understood if the ventures and networks of the entrepreneur are studied over space and time.

By definition entrepreneurship is risky; not all environments can be successfully enacted in spite of both internal and network resources. There are many reasons why this may be the case. Firstly, the own capabilites, including social, i e network, resources, may be limited. Secondly, the venture may oppose "objectified" areas where well-established images of reality, promoted by powerful actors, dominate. Thirdly, competing actors and their enactments may invade the same action field. If these threats to successful enactment as well as the personal network's natural ability to build further networks are recognized, the resulting hypothesis will be that entrepreneurs promote several parallel ventures.

The entrepreneur's personal network thus provides a tool by which to overcome mistakes and to practice experiential learning. While physical and financial resources are reduced through consumption, competences remain and may even grow if used in different ventures or if shared with outsiders. The potential of socioeconomic networks even increases through networking.

Management of Ambiguity

Management of ambiguity is now proposed to include the recognition, reduction, creation and balance of ambiguity.

Ambiguity has to be recognized with respect to form and content. Equivocalness as a state of the arts in the sense that lived experience calls for continuous interpretation and reinterpretation by every individual, is within a subjectivist approach considered to be natural. A famous Swedish entrepreneurial banker stated in an interview: the only way to deal with change is change. Meyerson and Martin (1986) propose ambiguity recognition as the major element in a viable corporate culture. It must be accepted that "reality" is a phenomenon that becomes redefined by individuals as they reflect upon history, live in the present and search for the future. New actors with different life worlds are brought into the enacted environment by way of the evolving network that is only partially controlled by the focal actor. An elaborate network will on the one hand thus provide the entrepreneur with social support for the defence of own ideas, on the other continuously provide reminders that alternative interpretations of the situation are abundant.

The general outlook has to be combined with an ability to identify changing perceptions, the exploitation of which will match own unique competence. Alternatively, established entrepreneurs have to be able to foresee emerging ambiguities in the marketplace whose exploitation will enforce the existing operations of the firm (cf Kirzner 1973). Again there is a need for a resourceful network comprising both weak and strong ties aimed at widening the range of the scanning operations and supporting the carrying out of intended actions.

Once ambiguity has been recognized it has to be moulded, i e competing interpretations of the environment have to be sorted out - for two major reasons. Firstly, then the entrepreneur or "ambiguity manager" can arrive at the conviction necessary to initiate action and associated enactment and learning processes. Secondly, actors within and without the business must be provided with "meaningful" interpretations of the environment, cf the introductory section. The entrepreneur then needs the pursuasive power to convince others about this image of reality and required appropriate action. Intuitive selection of problem solutions and opportunities will increase commitment and reduce perceived uncertainty and subsequently promote action, cf Brunsson, 1985.

As indicated above, entrepreneurs sometimes have to create room for enacting their vision. Where existing mental structures are cemented, a successive reorientation may not suffice. A revolution is needed. By infusing chaos, equivocalness and thus discretion is made available. "Crises awareness" will mobilize emotional and mental energy and incite people to question taken-for-granted structures. This ambiguity-creating strategy can be adopted within organizations as well as on the market. In the former case the outcome is a stronger position for the entrepreneur, whether owner-manager or corporate entrepreneur. Acquisition may be a means by which to make customers and competititors more willing to cooperate.

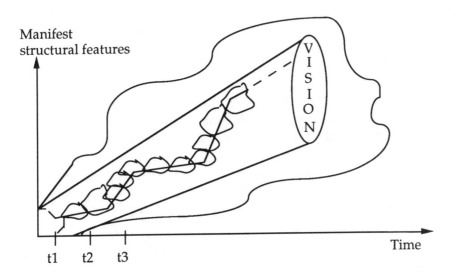

Figure 2. Balancing Change and Stability in the Entrepreneurial Career

In Figure 2 I try to illustrate the kind of "footprints" requried for the balancing of stability and change or rather interpretation and re-interpretation of events, actions and transactions in the environment. The trajectory depicts the manifested development of an entre–preneurial career, the broken lines available options, cf Figure 1 and Johannisson, 1981. The entrepreneur's vision guides the evolving career, cf Mintzberg, 1973, Normann, 1977. Originating in a vague setting (represented by the minor "cloud" at the origin), the venture/career, once off the ground, needs a definite course in order to reduce ambiguity and increase commitment for the various parties involved in the initiative. This means that recorded needs for adaptation down the road have to be "stored" if uncontrollable oscillations are to be avoided. The personal network of the entrepreneur must be able to provide the major part of this storage capacity. When the entrepreneur considers the reframing of the situation, appropriate, accumulated experiences are moulded into a seemingly discrete re-orientation of the trajectory. The process is perpetuated as the entrepreneurial career evolves in an evolutionary way, quite in contrast to the interpretation provided by Mintzberg, 1973. (Cf also Stevenson & Gumpert, 1985). The general turbulence of the socially constructed reality of the entrepreneur is illustrated with the large "cloud" that embeds the venturing process.

Outsiders thus usually perceive the entrepreneurial career to be discontinuous. It is reduced into a broken line where the breaks indicate strategic changes (Mintzberg, 1973). This argumentation is close to images of individual and organizational learning as proposed by Argyris & Schön, 1978. The "miniclouds", where venture transitions take place - cf Figure 1 - and the career line breaks, represent situations where double-loop learning takes place, intermittently supplementing the single-loop learning (the linear sections in between). Awareness of the turbulent setting for any learning process (the large "cloud") and appropriate action reveals ability to manage deutero-learning processes, i e capability to synchronize single- and second-loop learning processes.

The personal network includes caring ties as well as relationships that create the tensions needed if entrepreneurs are to activate double-loop learning processes. Elsewhere I have argued that condensations of entrepreneurial networks into "organizing contexts" will enforce learning capabilities. The enactment process will then be more manageable. However, in order not to obstruct the venturing process of the egocentric entrepreneur, support must be restricted to voluntary and organic completion of own resources and competences. If that is not the case there is an obvious risk that the support structure introduces a filter instead that misguides the entrepreneur's enactment process.

To conclude, competences for ambiguity management include ability to turn

* threats and mistakes into opportunities - to realize that while harmony and successes only confirm the present strategy, tension mobilizes energy and mistakes provide learning opportunities.

* competetive ties into cooperative ones - to realize that well-established opponents are well-informed and thus share your reality and that you may therefore make good partners, with mutually intelligible ideologies.

* paradox into reflection and curiosity - to realize that entre-preneurship like any creative activity means dealing with contradiction.

Conclusion: Recognizing Transaction Benefits

The arguments presented above merge into a major conclusion with respect to external control of entrepreneurship: entrepreneurs must design their own career by way of their personal network and disconnected from existing formal structures. Only then can they contribute to ambiguity reduction for themselves and others. This explains why "skunkwork" is considered to be inconceivably successful (Peters & Waterman 1982, Quinn 1988) while corporate entrepreneurship in terms of designed programmes to promote "intrapreneurship" have to manage paradox. A "laissez-faire" policy within clearly defined limits in this perspective appears to be the appropriate strategy for promoting entrepreneurship, whether through business policy in corporate settings or industrial policy in community settings. The suggested management principle is "management by opportunity", realizing that renewal can only be brought about by way of releasing human creativity through encouraging environmental exchange. Within this perspective it is meaningless to state short-termed objectives for policies aiming at stimulating entrepreneurship - whether in corporate or public settings.

Above I have introduced the notion of "organizing context" as the vehicle through which the entrepreneur's enactment of reality is facilitated and ambiguity management enforced. Obviously this context must be self-selected by the entrepreneur if her/his capabilites are to be fully exploited. The context's role of help for self-help remains however a delicate matter but this is not the only paradox within the field of entrepreneurial studies - they are abundant (Johannisson & Senneseth 1990).

In Section 2 I presented alternative network approaches to economic organization. The transaction-cost approach introduced by Williamson (1979) has therein been a common denominator, whether its framework is used as a platform or positioned against. This has produced many studies using axioms on instrumentality and decision rationality and providing conceptual and empirical conclusions that explain stability in business relationships and structures. The social dimension of the exchange is either rationalized and integrated into the framework or declared pathological. Action is seen as implementation of decision. The major difference between the framework concerning entrepreneurship provided here and that of proponents of industrial economics and marketing concerns the notion of a "transaction". While the latters' market actors are expected to associate transactions only with costs for settlement of an agreement between the exchanging parts, entrepreneurs in my framework also consider the "benefits" that exchange implies. These transaction benefits include:

*   being intrinsically motivated by the act of creation, entrepreneurs find stimulation in combining the varying and challenging "material" that the network provides;

*   resources externally supplied increase the variability needed to match the changing own perceptions of the environment and own preferences;

*   external exchange will significantly increase the opportunities for serendipitously initiated ventures.

Thus, structures aiming at reducing transaction costs and uncertainty, whether hierarchies or networks, will hamper the continuous organizing process that defines the evolving entrepreneurial career. The entrepreneur will structure activities by way of her/his personal network, thereby trading on resources such as personal commitment and naturally maintaining awareness of environmental equivocalness. Consequently, as manager of ambiguity the entrepreneur does not only contribute to the creation of future realities for other market actors but directs the making of her/his own identity as well.

References

Argyris, C., and Schön, D. A., (1978), Organizational Learning: A Theory of Action Perspective, Reading, Ma.: Addison Wesley.

Berger, P. L. and Luckmann, T., (1966), The Social Construction of Reality, New York, N.Y.: Doubleday.

Bouwen, R. and Steyaert, C., (1990), Construing Organizational Texture in Young Entrepreneurial Firms, Forthcoming in Journal of Management Studies.

Brunsson, N., (1985), The Irrational Organization. Irrationality as a Basis for Organizational Action and Change, New York, N.Y.: Wiley.

Brytting, T., (1991), Organizing in the Small Growing Firm, Stockholm School of Economics.

Burrell, G. and Morgan, G., (1979), (1988), Sociological Paradigms and Organisational Analysis, Aldershot: Gower.

Carland, J. W., Hoy, F. and Carland, J. A. C., (1988), "Who is an Entre-preneur?" Is a Question Worth Asking, American Journal of Small Business, Spring, pp 33-39.

Chell, E., (1985), The Entrepreneurial Personality: A Few Ghosts Laid to Rest? International Small Business Journal, Vol 3, No 3, pp 43-54.

Csikszentmihalyi, M., (1985), Reflections on Enjoyment, Perspectives in Biology and Medicine, Vol 28, pp 489-497.

Czarniawska-Joerges, B. and Wolff, R., (1989), Leaders, Managers, Entrepreneurs on and off the Organizational Stage, Research Paper 6389, Stockholm: EFI, HHS.

Drucker, P., (1985), Innovation and Entrepreneurship, New York: Harper & Row.

Gartner, W. B., (1989), "Who is an Entrepreneur?" Is the Wrong Question, Entrepreneurship Theory and Practice, Summer, pp 47-68.

Håkansson, H. (Ed.), (1982), International Marketing and Purchasing of Industrial Goods. An Interaction Approach, Chichester: Wiley.

Johannisson, B., (1983), Swedish Potential of the Evidence of Local Entrepreneurship in Regional Development, European Small Business Journal, Vol 1,2, pp 11-24.

Johannisson, B., (1987), Anarchists and Organizers - Entrepreneurs in a Network Perspective, International Studies of Management and Organization, Vol XVII, No 1, pp 49-63.

Johannisson, B., (1988), Business Formation - A Network Approach, Scandinavian Journal of Management, Vol 4, No 3/4, pp 83-99.

Johannisson, B., (1989), Beyond Industrial Policy - Cultural and Social Dimensions of Small Business Contexts, Paper presented at the 16th Annual Conference of the European Association for Research in Industrial Economics, Budapest 29 August - 1 September 1989.

Johannisson, B., (1990), Building an Entrepreneurial Career in a Mixed Economy: Need for Social and Business Ties in Personal Networks, Paper presented at the Academy of Managment Annual Meeting, San Francisco, USA, August 12-15, 1990.

Johannisson, B., (1990a), Economies of Overview - Guiding the External Growth of Small Firms, International Small Business Journal, Vol 9, No 1, pp 32-44.

Johannisson, B. and Senneseth, K., (1990), "Paradoxes of Entrepreneurship, Paper presented at the 4th Workshop on Recent Research in Entrepreneurship, Cologne, Germany, November 29-30 1990.

Johannisson, B. and Spilling, O. R. (Eds), (1986), Lokal naeringsutvikling - entreprenörskap og nettverksstrategier i noen norske og svenske kommuner, Oslo: Universitetsforlaget.

Kanter, R. Moss, (1972), Commitment and Community, Cambridge, Ma.: Cambridge University Press.

Kirzner, I. M., (1973), Competition and Entrepreneurship, Chicago, Ill.: The University of Chicago Press.

Koestler, A., (1964), The Act of Creation, London: Hutchinson.

Kolb, D. A ., Rubin, I. M. and McIntyre, J., (1984), Organizational Psychology - An Experiental Approach, Third edition, Englewood Cliffs, N.J.: Prentice-Hall.

Kylén, B., (1989), Hur företagschefer beslutar innan de blir överraskade (How CEOs Decide Before Being Surprised), Dissertation (English summary), Stockholm: Stockholm School of Economics.

Lessem, R., (1984), The Gestalt of Action Learning, In: Cox, C & Beck, J (Eds.), Management Development: Advances in Practice and Theory, New York, N.Y.: Wiley, pp 223-250.

March, J. G., (1976), The Technology of Foolishness, In: March, J. G. and Olsen, J. P., Ambiguity and Choice in Organizations, Oslo: Universitetsforlaget, pp 69-81.

March, J. G. and Olsen, J. P., (1976), Ambiguity and Choice in Organizations, Oslo: Universitetsforlaget.

Meyerson, D. and Martin, J., (1986), Questioning the Assumptions of Value Engineering: Alternative Views of the Cultural Change Process, In: the proceedings from The International Conference on Organizational Symbolism and Corporate Culture, Montreal, Juni 1986, Vol 1, pp 171-188.

Mintzberg, H., (1973), Strategy -Making in Three Modes, California Management Review, Vol XVI, No 2, pp 41-53.

Normann, R., (1977), Management for Growth, Chichester: Wiley.

Peters, T., (1988), Thriving on Chaos, New York, N.Y.: Harper & Row.

Peters, T. J. and Waterman, R. H., (1982), In Search of Excellence, New York, N Y: Warner.

Quinn, J. B., (1978), Strategic Change: Logical Incrementalism, Sloan Management Review, Fall, pp 1-28.

Quinn, J. B., (1988), Managing Innovation: Controlled Chaos, In: Quinn, J B et al, The Strategy Process, Englewood Cliffs, N.J.: Prentice Hall, pp 627-637.

Reuber, A. R., Dyke, L. S. and Fischer, E. M., (1990), Experientially Acquired Knowledge and Entrepreneurial Venture Success, In: the proceeding from the Academy of Management Annual Meeting, San Francisco, USA, August 12-15, 1990, pp 69-73.

Schumpeter, J. A., (1934), The Theory of Economic Development. Oxford: Oxford University Press.

Sjöstrand, S-E., (1986), The Dual Functions of Organizations, In: Johnsen, E (Ed.), Trends and Megatrends in the Theory of Management, pp 96-116.

Smircich, L. and Morgan, G., (1982), Leadership: The Management of Meaning, <u>Journal of Applied Behavioural Science</u>, Vol 18, No 3, pp 257-273.

Stevenson, H. H. and Gumpert, D. E., (1985), The Heart of Entrepre-neurship, <u>Harvard Business Review</u>, March-April, pp 85-94.

Thompson, J. D., (1967), Organizations in Action, New York, N.Y.: McGraw Hill.

Weick, K. E., (1979), The Social Psychology of Organizing, Reading, Ma.: Addison-Wesley.

Weick, K. E., (1984), Small Wins. Redefining the Scale of Social Problems, <u>American Psychologist</u>, January, pp 40-49.

Weick, K. E., (1976), Educational Organizations as Loosely Coupled Systems, <u>Administrative Science Quarterly</u>, Vol 21, pp 1-19.

Williamson, O. E., (1979), Transaction-Cost Economics: The Gover-nance of Contractual Relations, <u>Journal of Economics and Law</u>, Vol 22, pp 233-261.

Part 5

Changes in Information Technology

THE INTERPLAY BETWEEN DATA, TECHNOLOGY, DIALOGUES AND ORGANIZATIONAL EFFECTIVENESS

Kjell Grönhaug
Knut J. Ims
The Norwegian School of Economics and
Business Administration

Abstract

Firms adopt new information technologies to enhance their effectiveness. In this paper information technology is conceived as an integral part of the resources used by firms. To become more effective by adopting new information technologies they must be understood and applied in adequate ways. The important role of dialogues in creating an understanding that is of prime importance for designing and conducting valuable activities is highlighted.

Introduction

This paper focuses on the mediating role of dialogues for effective adoption and use of information technology to enhance organizational performance.

The field of data technologies is one of the major forces in shaping our lives. A distinction is made between "data" and "information". Data become information only after they have been sensed and interpreted. The new information technologies have impact on societies, influence the structuring and activities of organizations and have tremendous consequences for the individual. The importance of data technologies can hardly be overstated (cf Gerstein, 1987). A variety of points of

183

departure may be chosen when focusing on the new technologies. They may be studied from a technological, societal, organization, group or an individual perspective. Moreover, different themes such as adoption, use or changes due to the new technologies may be emphasized.

Our point of departure is the organization, or more precisely the business firm, and the important role played by competent, interacting organization members to benefit from the new technologies. There are several reasons for this choice. Firstly, an important part of the societal value creation takes place in business firms (which constitute on important subset of organizations, cf Dill, 1965). Secondly, for the individual business firms represents job opportunities, income, consumption possibilities, as well as challenges. Thirdly, well–run business firms reward owners and allow for taxes of importance for the execution of public programs of value to the society and its members.

Organizations

Organizations – and thus business firms – may be conceived of as "open systems". According to the open system metaphor organizations depend on the environments in which they are embedded and influence their environments as well. Organizations must be effective to survive and prosper (cf Aldrich, 1979). Effectiveness is an external standard related to the organizational ability to create acceptable outcomes to their constituencies, e g customers and owners in such a way that sufficient resources are retained allowing for survival and growth (Pfeffer and Salancik, 1979, p 11).

Organizations are assumed to exhibit purposeful, i e goal-directed behavior, which is consistent with the effectiveness assumption. What organizations do largely determine whether they succeed or fail. The organizational doing is reflected in its (the organization's) value activities (cf Porter 1985). To conduct value activities is costly, and competence, i e knowledge and skills, are needed to perform such activities properly. For the business firm choice and performance of value activities as reflected in its product and services are of the utmost importance. The customers represent an important – often the most important – external constituency for the firm. How the firm's product/service offerings are appreciated by its customers, and how they stand the comparisons of those offered by its competitors is critical, as business firms must cover their costs (at least in the long run) in order to stay in business, and as there is little doubt that excess profit is desirable.

Organizations consist of people. The individual is the "building block" in any organization. The various value activities are conducted by individuals. Thus the skills, knowledge and motivation of the individual will influence the organizational performance. In organizations over a certain minimum size, division of labor prevails. Organizations develop structures, and they operate technologies. For the organization, it is important that the activities of the individual organization members are coordinated, as the concerted effort of the organization is needed if to reach its best performance (cf Drucker, 1973) (given that the activities conducted are those appreciated by its customers and other external constituencies).

Knowledge and Rationality

To act purposefully presupposes rationality, which requires knowledge. The individual organization member must know the purpose of his activities, what activities to perform, how to perform them and how these activities relate to the activities of other organization members – and when the activities may need to be changed – as the organization as such is embedded in ever-changing environments. Man is, however, not omniscient. The most prevailing assumption in contemporary social sciences is probably that of limited cognitive capacity, i e man has limited capacity to seek, store, handle and make sense of (understand) data. The assumption of limited capacity has several implications. One is as reflected in Simon's (1957) notion of "bounded rationality", that:

" ..., the behaviors exhibited by the actors are intendedly rational, but only limited so" (p xxiv).

A similar notion is that of "satisfying behavior" (March and Simon, 1958), suggesting that actors do not consider the complete set of alternatives, nor their associated consequences, but stop their search for and evaluation of alternatives when an "acceptable" alternative has been found. The notions of "bounded rationality" and "satisfying behavior" both imply goal-directed behaviors, which (interpreted narrowly) assume that goals precede search for, evaluation of, and choice among alternatives. The assumption of limited cognitive capacity also allows for "irrational behavior", as actions may precede goals as emphasized for example in the literature on retrospective rationality (cf Shaw, 1980).

In order to act purposefully, the actor must understand his surrounding environments, i e the actor must understand the internal organizational environment and the organization as a collectivity must understand the external environment in which it is embedded. Why understanding is needed, is due to the fact that choice of goals and tasks, and the performance of activities can not be done in a vacuum, i e they are context-specific. Thus to operate in a rational way, i e to act purposefully, contextual rationality is needed (cf March, 1978, p 592). Contextual knowledge alone is, however, not sufficient. The actor must know how to determine goals and task, how to search for and evaluate activities, and how to perform the various activities. Thus also procedural rationality is needed (cf Simon 1978, p 8).

The notions of procedural and contextual rationality can be conceived as representing different types of knowledge, as reflected in Anderson's (1983) distinction between procedural and declarative knowledge. Procedural knowledge refers to appropriate rules and procedures, which can be applied for generating behaviors. Declarative knowledge is facts about events, things, their relations and states of the world, of crucial importance for interpretation and understanding the actual domain, where the procedural knowledge is supposed to be applied.

Studies of experts show that compared to novices they have much more elaborate cognitive structures (see Sanford 1987 for an excellent overview). Moreover, an important part of their knowledge-base is declarative knowledge acquired through experience, enabling them to act – in most cases – better than do the novices. Superiority in knowledge is important of several reasons. The open system metaphor employed here suggests that the relative performance of the organization is crucial, as the organizational doing reflected for example in the market place is compared with the activities of the firm's competitors. What really counts is how the organizational activities (as reflected in their product/service offerings) stand these comparisons. Moreover, superiority in knowledge may definetely represent a competitive advantage, as it allows the firm to make better decisions and to perform superior activities.

Technology

Any organization operates some sort of technology. The concept of technology is, however, an ambigous one. Three uses of the technology concept have been prevalent in the social sciences, i e as "apparatus, machines, and other physical devices"; as "techniques, the behaviors and cognitions that complete an instrumental act"; and as "a specific arrangement of persons, materials, and tasks" (Barley, 1990, p 64). Independent of how the concept of technology is (or has been) used, the following should be noted:

(1)   Organizations acquire and develop technologies to obtain some– thing, whatever it is. Acquisition and development of technolo– gies may thus be conceived as purposeful behavior, i e as means– end relationships. In everyday language, this may indicate that technology can be understood as "ways of doing things to reach some goal", or as emphasized by Merrill (1968): "Technologies are bodies of skills, knowledge, and procedures for making, using, and doing useful things" (p 576, our italics).

(2)   The technologies operated by the organization is related to the various value activities conducted by the firm. The activities performed determine the firm's position in the total value system and link it to its environments, e g suppliers and customers. Thus in using the generic value chain (Porter, 1985) as a point of depar– ture, it can be seen that the technologies operated by the firm

influence its inbound logistics, operations, outbound logistics, marketing and sales, and service operations, the linkages between the various activities, as well as retained margins. Choice and configuration of value activities, and how these activities are conducted are of crucial importance for the organizational competitiveness and performance as they greatly add to the positioning of the firm relative to its competitors and thus how its efforts are appreciated in the market place (cf Day and Wensley, 1988).

(3)   Technologies are operated by organization members. The skills and knowledge of these people, may be conceived as an important part of the organizational technology. When the technology is known, i e when the organizational members are experienced, they may be conceived as "experts" having command over the technology(-ies) they operate, i e they know "how to do things", they sense the limits and possibilities of the present technologies, and they are able to perform.

Information and Technology

The concept of 'information technologies' has been defined in several ways. Even though the definitions offered vary in width and scope, most of them emphasize the gathering, storage, transformation, dissemination and presentation of information (data) by use of computers, or as suggested by Gerstein (1987):

" ... the collective means to assemble and electronically store, transmit, process, and retrieve ..., as well as electronic means to control machines of all kinds, ..." (p 5).

Several things ought to be noted, such as :

(1)   Most definitions of information technologies emphasize specific physical characteristics of these technologies. The fact that the human understanding of and command over these technologies

188

are crucial for their effectiveness, even though recognized in real life – in particular by (incompetent) users, is largely left out.

(2)   Acquisition of information technology is only a part of the total set of organization technologies.

(3)   Moreover, gathering, storage, dissemination of information (data) takes place in any organization. Thus adoption of new information technology implies some change in the organizational information technology.

(4)   The organizational adoption of the new information technologies may be conceived as purposeful behavior to obtain something, e g reduced costs, to obtain better coordination, or to get updated information more rapidly.

Whether the adoption of new information technologies results in competitive advantages depends on a variety of factors, such as: The new technologies must be superior to the information technology presently used by the firm; they must be understood and integrated with the other organizational technologies, and they must be used properly. The organization should also be superior in adopting, integrating and using the new information technologies compared to its competitors! The last point is important as if the firm is less competent in adoption, integration and use of the new technologies then are its competitors, the new technologies will represent no competitive advantage, but only be related to the speed with which the firm is lagging behind.

To adopt something new represents change. Knowledge is needed to make adequate choices of what to adopt and to adjust the new informational technology to the current organizational context and use. Thus re–innovation will usually be crucial to achieve the intented purpose of increased competitiveness. This has been recognized by Rogers and Agarwala-Rogers (1976), who claim that:

"..... many innovations go through extensive tensions, essentially amounting to "reinventing" in the process of adoption and implementation" (p 159).

Moreover, as an innovation represents something new, and as it is partly unknown to the adopter, opting for new information technologies is risky. The risks involved are of different kinds, such as: Will the new technology work as expected (technological risk); can the new information technology be adopted and adjusted within the budgetary constraints (economic risk); and will the new technology enhance performance as expected (commercial risk) (cf Mansfield, 1981)? During the history of modern information technologies, adopting firms repeatedly have experienced the various types of risks – often with disastrous consequences, such as: The technology adopted have not worked as expected, have become operative only after considerable amount of time and frustrations; actual costs have by far exceeded calculated costs. (Studies conducted among Norwegian firms indicate that they only consider approximately 20 per cent of the real costs when acquiring information technology devices, leading to economic problems detoriating their economic performance. For detailed report, see Grønhaug & Ims,1990). The new technology have not resulted in the expected performance improvement.

Innovations, Value Activities and Competitiveness

New information technologies are adopted by organizations to gain relative advantages. To adequately assess the advantages requires relevant knowledge. Such knowledge is needed for example to assess how compatible the new technology is with the present organizational technologies and competencies, and to assess the needed changes to benefit from the technology adoption. (The vast literature on diffusion of innovations demonstrates that perceived relative advantages and compatibility with the present knowledge and behaviors are crucial determinants in the adoption decision (cf Rogers, 1983)).

Uncertainty

From this discussion it follows that adoption of the new information technologies is associated with uncertainty for the following reasons.

Firstly, the novelty of such technologies represents a major source of uncertainty. The rapid rate of change within the field of information technology escalate the uncertainty problem. Secondly, due to limited cognitive capacity constraints (as emphasized above) it is almost impossible to consider and evaluate all possible technology alternatives, and to assess with certainty their associated consequences to be realized in the future. In fact, the new technologies are more or less unknown, which makes it difficult to exhibit adequate behavior.

In order to benefit from the new information technologies, the organization must be aware of, understand and know how to use the new technologies and be able to make relevant changes to benefit from such investments. From the open system metaphor also follows that the organization must know its customers, their needs, and how they (the customers) will evaluate their product/service offerings – also when modified by new information technologies. The many voiced complaints, often leaving the customers with the feeling of being alinated and cause them to make "exit", i e stop being customers, indicate that this may be a serious problem. In a similar vein, the firm must know how adoption of new information technologies may affect its (the firm's) relationships with its suppliers and other relevant constituancies. In order to benefit from the new information technologies, the individual organization member affected must understand and possess the necessary knowledge and skills. Moreover, this understanding must be shared between the actors involved to coordinate the organizational activities to operate efficiently. Organization members vary in skills and motivation, as they vary in positions and tasks, which may highly influence their perceptions of, and attitudes and behaviors towards the new information technologies. This may make it difficult to arrive at the shared understanding needed of crucial importance to boost the organizational performance (cf Wilkins and Ouchi, 1983). For example, a common observation is that top management (i e the persons possessing the organizational top positions) who due to prior learning are stuck in "the competency trap" (cf March and Sproull, 1989), often turn their attention and interests away from the new technologies, which may definitely influence the firm's investment in, attention to and use of the new information technologies. (Our research demonstrates that computer illiteral managers represent a serious obstackle for adequate adoption and use of the new information technologies (Grønhaug & Ims, 1990)).

As realized advantages of the new information technologies will be reflected in the firm's doing, i e the value activities of prime importance for its competiveness, the potential advantages can be related to its (the firm's) value chain.

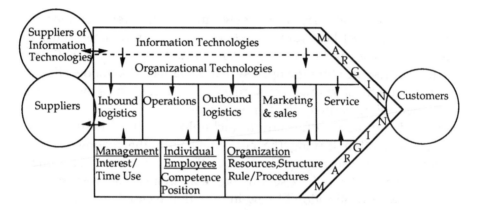

Figure 1. New Information Technologies and Value Creation

In figure 1 the primary activities, i e inbound logistics, operations, outbound logistics, marketing and sales, and service are placed in the middle of the traditional value chain (Porter, 1985). The technologies operated by the organization influence the various types of activities conducted. Adoption of new information technology will impact the other organizational technologies, and influence the primary activities in various ways. In fact, realized competitive advantages by adopting information technology are obtained by transforming the firm's value chain, and thus its primary activities (cf Porter and Millar, 1985).

As emphasized above, however, the competence of the individual organization member, and his understanding and use of the new technologies are of crucial importance to bring about the intended competive advantages of these technologies. As organizations consist of several members the collective understanding and use of the new

192

devices are crucial. A variety of factors related to the organizational setting, e g available resources, its structure, rules and procedures – and changes needed – to benefit from the new technologies, may impact both the speed and the extent to which the firm will be able to realize the intended advantages, as will top management's interests in and focus on the new information technologies. As adoption of new information technologies changes the firm's value creation, understanding of customers needs and how the changes are appreciated by them are important, as is the understanding of how adoption of new information technologies will influence the firm's relationships with suppliers and other constituencies. Of crucial importance is also knowledge of and sufficient competence to interact with suppliers of information technologies enabling the firm to choose, adopt and modify the adopted technology adequately. The importance of knowledge in order to interact with exchange partners, and adequately adopt new technologies has for long been recognized in the innovation literature. Dosi (1988) has stated this in the following way:

" ..... one needs have substantial inhouse capacity in order to recognize, evaluate, negotiate, and finally adapt the technology potentially available from others" (p 1132).

Moreover, the speed with which the firm act (which is to be related to adequate knowledge), is of importance for its competitiveness, as time is limited to get "first mover's advantage", and options seldom last for ever (see Eisenhardt, 1990 for an interesting discussion).

Problems and Understanding

To adopt and use new information technologies can be considered as purposeful, goal-directed behavior as emphasized at the outset of this paper. Such behavior can be conceived of as problem-solving. Problems are, however, not given realities, they must be discovered (see Dillon 1982 for an enlightening discussion). Indicators of problems are sensed, they are interpreted, and thus problems are created in the mind of the actor. An important point is that in situations perceived as complex, which often will be the case when confronted with the new information technologies, the actual problem will seldom (or never) be completely understood. The problem – or more correctly the problem-space – will only gradually be uncovered. Very often the problem perceived will beuseful solutions, common understanding is needed. From Figure 1 it is evident that common understanding is needed between organizational members, as it is in interactions with customers, suppliers and other constituencies. Because the individual actor creates her or his social reality (cf Berger and Luckman 1967), which is influenced by the actual social context of the actor as reflected in the seminal study reported Dearborn and Simon (1958), demonstrating that positions possessed and activities engaged in direct the attention of organizational members and problems perceived. Problem perceptions may vary substantially both between actors from the same organization (firm) as between actors across organizations. The common observation that "it is impossible to talk", or "we don't understand each other" exactly reflects that problems are perceived differently.

To create a common understanding, and thus the needed background for the concerted organizational effort, adequate problem definition is needed. This can be conceived as an informational problem. The appearant success of Japanese firms is partly attributed to their mode of decision-making emphasizing consensus, i e common understanding (Ouchi 1982).

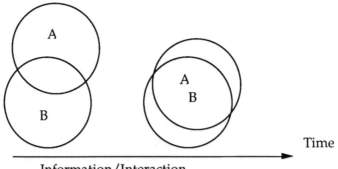

Figure 2. Interaction, Time and Problem Perception

Figure 2 illustrates the problem perceived by two actors, A and B. Due to different perspectives, e g differences in knowledge and factors emphasized, they differ in their problem perceptions. Through exchange of information, which takes time, they gradually arrive at similar perceptions of the actual problem, i e they understand each other. The striped circles also indicate that at the beginning perceptions of the problem are ambigous, while the complete circles indicate that they arrive of their confident, unambigous problem perceptions as interaction and exchange of information take place. Ambiguous problem perceptions are common, such as when the firm believes that the customer's problem is "X", while the customer perceive the problem to be "Z", which may cause dissatisfaction and inadequate and costly actions.

Dialogues and Information Richness

The prime value of information is its ability to reduce uncertainty and to clarify ambiguities. The organization´s ability to adopt, integrate and benefit from the new informtion technologies largely depend on its ability to process information. Information - or more correctly data - are mediated through a variety of media channels, e g advertisements and brochures, printed computer outputs, written documents, personal letters, telephone and face-to-face communication. The various media channels differ, however, highly in information richness; i e their ability to convey information (cf Daft & Lengel 1984). For the organization, choice of information channels is of utmost importance as the relative costs vary across media channels, i e the higher is the media richness, the higher are the relative costs to expose a given message. For example, it is less expensive to convey a simple message by using radio or a formal memo, than it is by using face-to-face communication.

When problems are novel and perceived as complex, media that are high in information richness are the most adequate. A common observation is that top-management has a preference for informal information through personal sources (for detailed discussion, see March and Sproull 1989). Face-to-face communication is very high in information richness as messages are designed and modified to the receiver, and it allows for immediate feedback. Face-to-face force communication also makes use of different types of information, e g spoken language, body language and demonstrations, i e it allows for exchange of complete audio-visual (-smell) information in the presence of others.

The dialogue can be conceived as a sub-set of personal, face-to-face communication. People use different everyday languages – and they play language-"games". Face-to-face communication is an effective means for developing and using the same language, and thus enhance common understanding (cf Phillips, 1977). Dialogues can be characterized as "conversations between two or more persons" or "exchange of ideas" (The Random House Dictionary). Key characteristics of the good dialogue are willingness to listen, to accept each other, to understand, and to explore the problems under scrunity.

In the context of the new information technologies dialogues are of crucial importance to enhance understanding, and thus of importance for beneficial adoption and use of the new technologies. Dialogues, through asking and listening, allows for the testing of assumptions, reduction of uncertainty, problem discovery, and the construction of adequate solutions.

In returning back to Figure 1, it is easily seen that the information technologies adopted that must be understood to be operated effectively. Integration of the new information technology with the other organizational technologies, and adjustments to the various primary value activities, the problems confronted with are multiple. In a similar vein the firm may be confronted with multiple challenges to establish the most effective relationships with suppliers and customers, and other constituencies, when adopting new information technologies changing its value activities.

Learning-by-doing is important in adoption of the new and complex information techniques and software included may be considered as important part of this technology. From an organizational point of view, the adjustments needed and acquisition of knowledge and skills are equally important, indicating that effective exchange of information is crucial. The complexity of new technologies, and the importance of adequate information exchange for effective technology transfer have also been recognized by others, e g as stated by Teece (1980),

"... the human capital in an effective team configuration accompany the transfer" (p 241).

The importance of understanding the customers is emphasized throughout the marketing literature. In the same way as the firm may hold ambiguous problem perceptions about the customers, the customer's understanding of their own problems may be ambiguous. Even worse, customers often don't know their own problems, and thus they don't know how they should be solved.

".. buyers often have a difficult time assessing it (the firms product offerings) in advance. Buyers then, ... often do not know what they should look for ..." (Porter, 1985, p 138).

The importance of dialogues with customers has been studied by von Hippel (1988). His research shows that the firm and its customers arrive at new ideas and develop new products together through dialogues. The common observation that long-lasting relationships exist between the firm, its suppliers and customers reflects the fact that time is needed to arrive at a common understanding. Such knowledge is partly context specific and tacit in nature. It should also be noted that the context specific and tacit knowledge embedded in long-lasting relationships (as well as between organizational members within and across or-ganizations) is an important, but often overlooked asset to the firm, termed as "social capital" by Coleman (1988) to capture the value of joint knowledge (and trust) in such relationships.

Challenges and Promises

The complexity of the new information technologies, and the difficulties involved in making good use of their potential in the organizational value creating activities (cf Figure 1) have repetitively been emphasized throughout this paper. Time and learning challenges are needed to benefit from the new information technologies to gain competitive advantages. Exposure to challenging problems is important as the individual's attention span is limited. In order to get command over the new information technologies, the firm and the individual user must be exposed to new problems enhancing learning of new skills to acquire superior knowledge. Informational networks allowing for dialogues with technology suppliers, customers, and competent collegues, are important of several reasons. Without new challenges, there are no incentives for new learning, and thus after a certain period of time the organizational learning will decline. Decline in learning will cause decline in competitiveness as the firm is embedded in everchanging environments. The domain of new information technologies develops very rapidly. In order to enhance the organizational competitiveness, continous upgrading (Porter, 1990), i e adoption and integration of new solutions, and learning of new skills is needed. Adequate flow of information is a prerequisite for this to take place. Informational networks allowing for exposure to adequate problems and information, and access to dialogues with competent actors, is needed to enhance learning and change (cf Levitt and March 1988). To establish, develop and benefit from such informational networks represent challenges to management and employees, as continuous learning, work and upgrading are required. Being embedded in such informational and learning environments, however, also gives the promise of interesting challenges, rewards and the taste of success.

References

Aldrich, H.A., (1979), Organizations and Environments, New Jersey, Prentice-Hall.

Anderson, J.R., (1983), The Architecture of Cognition, Cambridge MA: Harvard University Press.

Barley, S.R., (1990), The Alignment of Technology and Structure through Roles and Networks, Administrative Science Quarterly, Vol 35, pp 65–103.

Berger, P.L. and Luckman T., (1967), The Social Construction of Reality, New York: Doubleday.

Coleman, J.S., (1988), Social Capital in the Creation of Human Capital, <u>Am. Journal of Sociology</u>, Vol 95, Supplement, pp 95 – 120.

Daft, R.L., Lengel, R.H., (1984), Information Richness: A New Approach to Managerial Behavior and Organization Design, In: L.L. Cummings and B. Staw (eds.), Research in Organizational Behavior, Vol 6, Greenwich, C.T., JAI Press, pp 191–233.

Day, G.S. and Wensley, R., (1988), Assessing Advantage: A Framework for Diagnosing Competitive Superiority, <u>Journal in Marketing</u>, Vol 52 (April), 1–20.

Dearborn, D.C. and Simon H.A., (1958), Selective Perception: A Note on Departemental Identification of Executives, <u>Sociometry</u>, Vol 21, pp 140–144.

Dill, W.R., (1965), Business Organizations, In: J.G. March (ed.), Handbook of Organizations, Chicago: Rand McNally, pp 1071–1114.

Dillon, D.T., (1982), Problem Finding and Problem Solving, <u>Journal of Creative Behavior</u>, Vol 16, No 2, pp 97–111.

Dosi, G., (1988), Sources, Procedures, and Microeconomic Effects of Innovation, <u>Journal of Economic Literature</u>, Vol XXVI (September), 1120–1171.

Drucker, P.E., (1973), Management, Task, Responsibilities, Practices, New York: Harper and Row.

Eisenhardt, K.M., (1990), Speed and Strategic Choice: How Managers Accelerate Decision Making, <u>California Management Review</u>, Vol 32, No 3 (Spring), 39–54.

Gerstein, M.S., (1987), The Technology Connection, Readding, MA: Addison-Wesley.

Grønhaug, K. and Ims, K.J., (1990), Datateknologi, informasjon og kon‐kurranseevne, Bergen Center for Applied Research, Norwegia Adm., Report no 13/90.

von Hippel E., (1988), Lead Users: A Source of New Product Concepts, In: K. Grønhaug and G. Kaufmann (eds.), Innovation: A Cross-Disciplinary Perspective, Oslo: Norwegian University Press, pp 387–406.

Levitt, B. and March J. G., (1988), Organizational Learning, Annual Review of Sociology, Vol 14 (manuscript).

Mansfield, E., (1981), How Economists See R & D, Harward Business Review, (November- December), pp 98–106.

March, J.G., (1978), Bounded Rationality, Ambiguity, and the Engi‐neering of Choice, Bell Journal of Economics, Vol 9, pp 587–608.

March, J.G. and Sproull, L.S., (1989), Technology, Management, and Competitive Advantage, In: PS. Goodman and L.S. Sproull (eds.), Technology and Organizations, San Fransisco, Jossey-Bass (manuskript).

Merill, R.S., (1968), The Study of Technology, In: D. E. Sills (ed.), International Encyclopedia of the Social Sciences, Vol 15, pp 576-586.

Ouchi, W.G., (1982), Theory Z. How American Business Can Meet the Japanese Challenge, New York: Avon Books.

Pfeffer, J. and Salancik G. R., (1979), The External Control of Organi‐zations, New York: Harper and Row.

Phillips, D.L., (1977), Wittgenstein and Scientific Knowledge, A Socio‐logical Perspective, New Jersey: Rowman and Littlefield.

Porter, M.E., (1985), Competitive Advantage, New York: Free Press.

Porter, M.E., (1990), The Competitive Advantage of Nations, New York: Free Press.

Porter, M.E. and Millar V. E., (1985), How Information Gives You Competitive Advantage, Harvard Business Review, (July-August), pp 25–36.

Rogers, E.M., (1983), Diffusion of Innovations, New York, The Free Press (3rd ed.).

Rogers, E.M., (1976), Communication in Organizations. Argarwala-Rogers, R. New York: The Free Press.

Sanford, A.J., (1987), The Mind of Man. Models of Human Under-standing, Brighton, Sussex: Harvester Press.

Simon, H.A., (1957), Administrative Behavior, New York: The Free Press, (2nd ed.).

Simon, H.A., (1978), Rationality as a Process and Product of Thought, American Economic Review, Vol 68, pp 1–16.

Staw, B.N., (1980), Rationality and Justification in Organizational Life, In: B.M. Staw and L.L. Cummings (ed.), Research in Organizational Behavior, Greenwhich, CT, JAI Press, Vol 2, pp 84–90.

Stein, J., (1980), The Random House Dictionary, New York: Ballantine Books.

Teece, D.J., (1980), Economies of Scope and Scope of Economics, Journal of Economic Behavior and Organization, Vol 1, pp 223–247.

Wilkins, A.L., Ouchi, W.G., (1983), Efficient Cultures: Exploring the Relationship between Culture and Organizational Performance, Administrative Science Quarterly, 28, pp 468–481.

CURRICULUM VITAE OF LUCA PACIOLI, 495 B SJ - 423 B SJ.

Alf Sandin
Gothenburg School of Economics and
Commercial Law

A Preamble

Last year Sten Jönsson (SJ) had survived 50 winters. This historical event in accounting naturally reminds us of another historical highlight - 500 years with Luca Pacioli.

Sten Jönsson is well known, but who was Luca Pacioli? By means of a reconstructed and somewhat commented curriculum vitae, let us become acquainted with him.

According to the old Christian calender, Luca Pacioli lived between 1445 and 1517. With 1940 as a new point of departure, we get 495 B SJ to 423 B SJ. During a transitional period we ought to use double-entry year-keeping. However, for the period we are accounting for, the old Christian calender will be used.

In spite of being a man of the church, a Franciscan, Luca Pacioli became a father. We know him as the father of double-entry book-keeping. Unfortunately, our accountants' knowledge of him ends there. However, he was important in other fields as well, as the following curriculum vitae will show.

Curriculum vitae

The spelling of his name is a story in itself. Here, he will simply be used one of two main possibilities in Toscana, Paciolo or Pacioli.

Born in 1445 (the exact year is uncertain) in the village of Borgo San Sepolcro in the Republic of Florence. The village, where he spent all his youth, was highly influenced by the Franciscan tradition. San Francisco had often stayed there on his journeys.

In 1460 began a deep friendship with the famous painter from the same village, Piero Della Francesca. Mathematics and science of proportions was important in art, and Fransesca, who was a master in these fields, taught them to Pacioli. The friendship with Fransesca also led him to contacts with the court of the Duke of Urbino. His taste for science was stimulated in the Duke's library. One of Luca's relatives, Benedetto, had taken part in the conquest of Naples. It is probably from him that Pacioli got his deep military knowledge.

At the age of 20, Pacioli left his village for a job as a tutor to Bartolo, Francesco and Paulo, the sons of a rich merchant, Antonio Pompiasi. He had to take part in many caravans of merchandise, and thereby received a business education.

His first manuscript

By the time he left the family Pompiasi in 1470 he dedicated his first work "De Veribus Quantitatis" to the three sons. This is a kind of predecessor to the "Summa..." and was followed by two others, one in Perugia in 1476 and another in Zara in 1481.

In Venice he listened to the public lectures on mathematics given by Doménico Bragadino.

In 1470 - 1471 Pacioli stayed in Rome. His master Piero was also there, called by the Pope to decorate the Vatican. He served again as an introducer to the high society circles, among others to the powerful family Della Rovere to whom belonged the future Pope Julio II. He became acquainted with persons interested in architecture.

About the year 1472 Luca Pacioli joined the Franciscan Order.

Piero Della Fransesca takes Pacioli as a model for Saint Peter in a famous painting. "La Madonna con Bambino, Santi e Angeli e il duca Frederico II da Montefeltro". This was the first portrait of Pacioli.

In 1475 Luca Pacioli was lecturer in mathematics in Perugia. Contract for two years. Because of his skill and fame he received higher wages than others. He stayed there an extra year.

After a short period in Florence he returned to Perugia, where he in 1486 (possibly in 1487) received the academic title "Magister" (doctorate) which gave him a right to become professor at the university.

In 1488 he left the university because of overwork and bad health and returned to Rome where he lived also in 1489.

In 1490 he taught theology and mathematics in Naples.

Preparation of the "Summa..."

From 1490 to 1493 he stayed in his native village to prepare the famous "Summa de Arithmetica Geometria Proportione et Proportionalitá", 616 pages. In that book we find the double-entry bookkeeping and that is why we know Luca Pacioli. Pacioli had now thus in fact written four books in the mathematical field.

Pacioli gave public lectures in aritmethic and geometry in Padua in 1493.

In the same year his superiors in the order forced him to go to Asis, threatening him with excommunication. It seems that his fellows in the order were jealous of his position as a free man and university lecturer. However, he was not excommunicated.

In 1494 he went to Venice to assist in the printing of the "Summa.." The significance of the book is suggested by the fact that it was one of the early books set by the movable type system invented by Gutenberg about 1450. After the publication of the "Summa..." he went back to Urbino in 1494, where he was met with great respect. A famous portrait from this time shows Pacioli explaining his theorems.

In 1496 he was invited by Duke Ludovico Sforza (also called Ludovioco il Moro) to teach mathematics in Milan. Leonardo da Vinci stayed there at the same time and they became very good friends.
As a result of this friendship Leonardo made seventy drawings for Pacioli´s new famous work, "De Divina Proportione", 1497.

In 1499 both had to leave Milan with the French occupation and the fall of Ludovico il Moro. They stayed for short periods in Mantua, Venice and Florence.

From 1500 - 1505 he taught at the universities of Pisa, Perugia, Bologna and Florence.

From 1505 - 1508 he stayed at the court of vice chancellor Galeotto Franciotti in Rome.

Special rights

In 1508 his old friend Giulano Della Rovere, who now had become Pope Julio II, gave him the right to own material assets, otherwise forbidden for Franciscans. This year he also wrote his first will and went on his last journey to Venice. There he held a lecture on Euclides for 500 persons in the church of San Bartolomeo.

He stayed in Venice until 1509, monitoring the printing of "De Divina Proportione" published in the same year.

In 1509 he returned to teach at the University of Perugia. His health was getting worse and he often had to ask his students for understanding and patience.

In 1510 he was nominated "Comisario" (Dean) at the monastery in his native village.

In 1511 he wrote a new will.

Pope León X requested him to be Professor of Mathematics and he went to Rome in 1514. News of Pacioli ends on August 30, 1514.

In 1517 Luca Pacioli died in his native village of Borgo San Sepolcro. For a long time the exact date was not known but recent research has established that it was 19 June.

Shortly after his death the fame of Luca Pacioli faded away. It was only in the middle of the nineteenth century that his work regained interest. With 1994 coming closer, we can expect a new wave of "Pacioliana".

More than accounting

What we seldom learn about Pacioli is his great importance in art and architecture through his work "De Divina Proportione". Probably every trainee in the graphical field, maybe without knowing, has come across the so-called Golden Section, Section d'Or, Goldener Schnitt, Gyllene snittet. This cannot be attributed to Pacioli. It was known by Pythagoras and developed by Plato. Maybe it was known also in Old China. But Paciolis´ "Divina Proportione" is still considered to be the most important book on the subject. In his work he elaborates on ideas from Plato, Euclides and others. With the help of Leonardo da Vinci he made the ideas visible and he developed them.

The Golden Section tells us that if a quantity is so divided that the ratio between the smaller part and the greater is the same as the ratio between the greater part and the whole, then it is divided according to the Golden Section. Mathematically the relation between the parts is $a/b = c/a$.

Pacioli called it "Divine" for various reasons. The proportion of the Golden Section is one and unique like God. It has three quantities like the Holy Trinity. Like God it can not be defined in common words. The relation between the parts is an irrational number, 1.618.... It is also eternal and unchangeable.

It is understandable why the Golden Section has received its fame. We find it in many cases in nature, in crystals and in bodies of animals and men. From the top of the head to the navel, and from the navel to the feet, we have an example of the Golden Section. In architecture for example Le Courbusier was guided by this principles which he called "Modulor" (Modul d'Or).

For this paper interviews have been made in Gothenburg with people in art and design. It seems that Pacioli is known more in detail in those circles than among accountants. It might be explained by the fact that he wrote the best book regarding the Golden Section and which has had a tremendous importance in art and architecture.

A call has also been made to the Department of Mathematics at the University of Gothenburg. The person who happened to answer the telephone immediately recognized Pacioli's name, in part because Pacioli in the "Summa..." concluded that there was no solution to a third degree equation. The solution was, however, found in the sixteenth century.

Concluding remarks

We know Pacioli as the father of double-entry bookkeeping. However, we also know that he was not the inventor. He writes himself in the accounting part of the "Summa..." "Particularis de Computis e Scripturis", 26 pages, that he simply describes the practice in Venice. With modesty he also points out that the "Summa..." is a compilation.

Pacioli has normally given references to many authors but we do not know how he learned the practice in Venice. There are speculations regarding this subject and maybe the intense interest in his person around the 500 year anniversary will give us more information about Pacioli - who was not even an accountant!

On a plaquett in his native village the citizens demand his forgiveness for being too long forgotten. It has been a privilege to give this small contrubution to his memory.

References

Haulotte, R. and Stevelinck, E., (1962), La vie et l'aeuvre de Luca Pacioli, Revue Belge de la Comptabilité, Bruxelles, 30 juin.

Haulotte, R. and Stevelinck, E., (1975), Luca Pacioli, Sa vie Son aeuvre, Vesoul: Pragnos.

Lindgren, J., (1975), Mått och proportioner, (Measures and Proportions), Gothenburg University, Konstindustriskolan.

Lindgren, J., (1979), Geometrisk komposition och design, DE PLATONSKA OCH GEOMETRISKA KROPPARNA (Geometrical Composition and Design THE PLATONIC AND GEOMETRICAL BODIES), Gothenburg University, Konstindustriskolan.

Pacioli, L., (1987), La Divina Proporción, Introducción de Antonio M. Gonzáles, Madrid: AKAL.

Persson, E., (1985), Den sköna geometrin, (The Beautiful Geometry), Stockholm: Gidlunds.

Stettler, Howard F., Comments on the Rationale Underlying Major Developments in the Allied Fields of Accounting and Auditing in the Middle East and Western World, University of Kansas, undated.

Stevelinck, E., (1982), Du nouveau sur Luca Pacioli, Bulletin de l'Institut National des Historiens Comptables de France, no 7.

About the authors

Olof Arwidi is Professor at the School of Economics, Lund University, Sweden. His research area is management accounting, planning and control, criteria and measurement. The main areas of publication are planning, inflation accounting, investment planning, translation of foreign accounts and management control.

Jacob G. Birnberg is Professor of Business Administration (Accounting) in the Katz Graduate School of Business of the University of Pittsburgh, USA. He also was a member of the faculty of the University of Chicago's Graduate School of Business. He has been a visiting faculty member at The London Business School and The Oxford Centre for Management Studies (now Templeton College). His research interests are primarily in the areas of management control systems and are behaviorally oriented.

Richard J. Boland Jr., is Professor of Information and Decision Systems and Professor of Accounting at the Weatherhead School of Management, Case Western Reserve University in Cleveland, Ohio, USA. Prior to joining the Weatherhead School, he was Professor of Accounting at the University of Illinois at Urbana-Champaign from 1976 through 1989. He spent 1988-89 as the Eric Malmsten Professor at the Gothenburg School of Business and Commercial Law. He is editor of the new international journal, *Accounting, Management and Information Technologies.*

Salvador Carmona is Associate Professor of Accounting at Universidad de Sevilla, Spain, where he has served as Chairperson of accounting. He has coauthored three books and edited another one. He is the associate editor of Cuadernos de Investigacion Contable.

Barbara Czarniawska-Joerges, is Professor of Business Administration at Lund University, Sweden. Her research focuses on control processes in complex organizations. She has published widely in the area of business administration in Polish, her native language, as well as in Swedish and English, including Controlling Top Management in Large

Organizations (1985), Ideological Control in Nonideological Organizations (1988), Economic Decline and Organizational Control (1989) and Exploring Complex Organizations: A Cultural Perspective (1992). Her articles have appeared in Economic and Industrial Democracy, Scandinavian Journal of Management, Organization Studies, Journal of Management Studies, Accounting, Organizations and Society, Management Communication Quarterly and Consultation.

Mahmoud Ezzamel, Ph.D. is currently the Price Waterhouse Professor of Accounting and Finance at the Manchester School of Management, University of Manchester Institute of Science and Technology (UMIST), England. Previosly, he has held positions at the University College of Wales, Aberystwyth, the University of Southampton, and Queen's university of Canada. He has published widely in the management accounting and financial analysis areas. His main research interests are the interface between management accounting and organizational control with particular emphasis on divisionalised companies and not-for-profit organizations, and financial statement analysis. He is an editorial board member of the *Journal of Business Finance and Accounting*.

Kjell Grønhaug is Professor of Business Administration at the Norwegian School of Economics and Business Administration. His publications include numerous articles in leading European and American journals, contributions to multiple conference proceedings, and he is the author or coauthor of 13 books. His present research interests relate to cognitive and economic aspects of corporate strategy, innovative behavior, and research methodology.

Isabel Gutierrez is Associate Professor of Organizational Behavior at Universidad de Sevilla, Spain. She has coauthered one book and published articles in the European Journal of Operational Research and in the Scandinavian Journal of Management.

Knut J. Ims is Associate Professor of Management Informations Systems at the Norwegian School of Economics and Business Administration. He has done extensive work on how managers make use of information and their perceptions, data security, the important role played by dialoges and business ethics. His present research focuses on data security, managerial cognition, understanding and dialogues.

Bengt Johannisson has his academic educational "roots" in Gothenburg, Sweden, where he in 1965 got his first degree at Gothenburg School of Economics. 1967-1974 he taught at Umeå University where he got a B.A. and Lic-degree in 1971. Since 1974 he works at Växjö University. In 1979 he was appointed Associated Professor (docent) at Lund University and in 1981 he presented his doctoral thesis at University of Gothenburg. In 1989 he got a chair at Roskilde University Center in Denmark and the same year he was appointed professor of Entrepreneurship and Business Development at Lund University. He has been abroad twice as a visiting research fellow, one year (1971/72) at Aston University, Birmingham, England and one year (1983/84) at York University, Toronto, Canada.

Rolf A. Lundin is Professor of Business Administration at the University of Umeå, Sweden, where he is also the Dean of the Business School. He has published work in Management Science and Organization Theory and he has served as the editor of Scandinavian Journal of Management Studies. His research interests as of today center on knowledge intensive firms and project organization of work. Currently he is working together with Hans Wirdenius on a book with the tentative title: "Organizing and Managing by projects: The European Approach".

Thomas Polesie is Associate Professor of Business Administration at the Gothenburg School of Economics and Commercial Law. His dissertation in 1976 analyzes some experience of management by objectives in 7 companies. "Human Factors in Budgeting - judgment and evaluation", carries on the theme of strategy with regard to a company's economic conditions - with Vagn Madsen. Then came a design study of a system for budgeting and accounting in the city of Uppsala - action and reaction. "Att beskriva företags ekonomi" (1989) takes up some issues that pertain to the craft of accounting and presents a comprehensive model for the design of accounting systems in different contexts. "Företag i förändring - en studie av identitet och ekonomi" appeared in 1990. It is a study of the evolution of 16 companies, manufacturers, system designers, ship yards, shipping companies and a trading house. This study has been extended with 2 new cases and further comparisons between the development paths of the different companies have been made. The study was published in 1991 as "Continuity and change - corporate identity in a Scandinavian perspective".

Alf Sandin is Assistant Professor at Gothenburg School of Economics and Commercial Law. He has written a thesis on "Risk management and risk information" and is coauthor of a book on the same subject. This year will also a book regarding the history of State accounting be published. A number of articles on accounting in various countries have been written for the journal of the Swedish auditors organisation.

Hugh C. Willmott, Ph. D. is currently Senior Lecturer in the School of Management, UMIST, Manchester, England, having previosly held positions at Aston University and Copenhagen Business School. He has published widely in social science, management and accounting journals. Presently he is engaged in research on accounting and auditing regulation, management control and the use of communication technologies. He is an editorial board member of *Accounting, Auditing and Accountability Journal, Advances in Public interest Accounting*, and *Critical Perspectives on Accounting*.